DISCO

INSIDE ISSUE 3: GENESIS, MARK,

1 Find a time when you can read the Bible each day

2 Find a place where you can be quiet and think

4 Ask God to help you understand what you read

3 Grab your Bible and a pencil or pen

5 Read today's Discover page and Bible bit

6 Pray about what you have read and learned

We want to...

- Explain the Bible clearly to you
- Help you enjoy your Bible
- Encourage you to turn to Jesus
- Help Christians follow Jesus

Discover stands for...

- Total commitment to God's Word, the Bible
- Total commitment to getting its message over to you

Team Discover

Martin Cole, Nicole Carter, Rachel Jones, Kirsty McAllister, Alison Mitchell, André Parker, Ben Woodcraft

Discover is published by The Good Book Company, Blenheim House, 1 Blenheim Rd, Epsom, Surrey, KT19 9AP, UK.
Tel: 0333 123 0880; Email: discover@thegoodbook.co.uk UK: thegoodbook.co.uk
North America: thegoodbook.com Australia: thegoodbook.com.au NZ: thegoodbook.co.nz

How to use Discover

Here at Discover, we want you at home to get the most out of reading the Bible. It's how God speaks to us today. And He's got loads of top things to say.

We use the New International Version (NIV) of the Bible. You'll find that the NIV and New King James Version are best for doing the puzzles in Discover.

The Bible has 66 different books in it. So if the notes say...

Read Genesis 25 v 19-26

...turn to the contents page of your Bible and look down the list of books to see what page Genesis begins on. Turn to that page.

"Genesis 25 v 19" means you need to go to chapter 25 of Genesis, and then find verse 19 of chapter 25 (the verse numbers are the tiny ones). Then jump in and start reading!

Here's some other stuff you might come across...

WEIRD WORDS

Quamtoff
These boxes explain baffling words or phrases we come across in the Bible.

Think!

This bit usually has a tricky personal question on what you've been reading about.

Action!

Challenges you to put what you've read into action.

Wow!

This section contains a gobsmacking fact that sums up what you've been reading about.

Pray!

Gives you ideas for prayer. Prayer is talking to God. Don't be embarrassed! You can pray in your head if you want to. God still hears you! Even if there isn't a Pray! symbol, it's a good idea to pray about what you've read anyway.

Coming up in Issue 3…

Jacob: Changed cheat

We begin in Genesis to meet Jacob — a man who started fighting with his twin brother when they were babies in their mother's womb! And the family arguments certainly didn't stop when they both grew up…

Jacob cheated his brother and his dad, bickered with his wives, and even wrestled with God! But despite all that, God had chosen Jacob to be part of his special plan for his people — and God doesn't give up on his plans! He blessed Jacob with an amazing dream of heaven, a HUGE family, massive wealth… and even turned this cheater into a changed man. Read all about it in Genesis!

Mark: Jesus the King

We catch up with Jesus in Mark's Gospel for the week before he dies — but Jesus still has a whole lot left to teach his disciples (and us!).

We'll watch as Jesus goes on an unusual donkey ride, throws over tables in the temple, reveals what the MOST IMPORTANT commandment is and even gives us a sneak preview of the end of the world!

Through it all, Mark, the author, will be showing us that Jesus is King and is in total control!

Acts: Spread the news

The book of Acts is certainly ACTion-packed (get it?). It's all about how Jesus' disciples (now called apostles) began to spread the gospel. The GOSPEL is the good news that Jesus died for us and was raised back to life — it's a life-changing message! And it certainly didn't go unnoticed when the apostles started talking about it. Lots of unexpected people believed the good news, but the apostles also got loads of hassle for talking about Jesus too.

Prepare yourself for journeys, jailbreaks and jaw-dropping… sermons (yes, really!).

Philippians: Joy for Jesus

Philippians is a letter written by the apostle Paul to the Christians in Philippi — in this issue of Discover we pick it up halfway through. Paul has some surprising things to say!

Knowing Jesus is what makes Paul really really happy — and he wants us to know that joy too! In fact, Paul even says that in comparison to Jesus, everything else is like… dog poo!

Don't believe it?
Read on and find out…

Jacob: Changed cheat

Genesis 25 v 19-26

In the last two issues of Discover, we've been reading the Genesis story.

It's all about God and His special people, the Israelites.

WEIRD WORDS

Aramean
Person from the country of Aram

Esau
Means *"hairy"*

Jacob
Means *"grab the heel"* and *"deceiver"*

Here are the highlights so far...

> God created **EVERYTHING**. (Genesis chapter 1)

> **Adam and Eve disobeyed God**, bringing sin into the world. (Chapter 3)

> **People continued to sin** against God, so He flooded the world to destroy His enemies. But God rescued Noah and his family. (Chapters 6-9)

> Noah's great, great, great (etc) grandson was Abraham. **God made three amazing promises to Abraham**. (Chapter 12)

1. LAND
God promised to give Abraham's family the country of Canaan.

2. CHILDREN
God would give Abraham loads of descendants. They became God's special people — the Israelites.

3. BLESSING
God promised to bless the whole world through Abraham's family. He would do this by sending Jesus.

Read Genesis 25 v 19-26 *and fill in the gaps.*

I_____ was Abraham's son. His wife R_____ was unable to have children (v21). But God had promised that Abraham and Isaac would have loads of descendants!

So Isaac p_____ to the Lord for a child (v21). God answered his prayer and Rebekah had twins! But they were enemies even while they were still in the womb!

God said that E_____ and J_____ would grow up to lead separate n_____ and the older one would serve the y_____ one (v23).

More about that tomorrow...

Isaac and Rebekah had to wait 20 years before they could have a child. But God not only kept His promise, He gave them twins!

Pray!

Thank God that He always keeps His promises. And that when we pray, He often gives us far more than we ask for.

2

Stewpid Esau

**Genesis
25 v 27-34**

Below, write the name of your brother or sister (if you haven't got any, scribble in a friend).

Now, in the larger box, describe how you're different from them.

WEIRD WORDS

Wild game
Animals that are hunted for food, like deer

Famished
Starving

Edom
It means *red*

Despised
Thought it was worthless

Read Genesis 25 v 27-28

Esau and Jacob were twins but were totally different from each other. Esau was a great hunter, but Jacob was far more sly...

Read verses 29-34

Who did what? Write an E for Esau, and a J for Jacob.

Was cooking lentil stew	J
Came in, starving	
Asked for some stew	
Asked for his brother's birthright	
Promised to hand over the birthright	
Gave his bro some stew	J

So what's the big deal?

BIRTHRIGHT = BIG DEAL

In those days, the oldest son was given the birthright. This meant that he would...

- inherit loads more than his brothers
- become head of the family when his father died

EVEN BIGGER DEAL

The birthright in this family was extra special because the oldest son would...

- inherit God's great promises to Abraham (see yesterday's *Discover*)
- become head of God's special family (the Israelites)

This really was a big deal. But Esau handed over the birthright to Jacob for a bowl of stew!

Think!

How do you treat what God has given you — family, friends, home, food, the Bible?
Are you grateful to God, or do you take it all for granted?

Remember what God promised Rebekah yesterday? *"The older son will serve the younger"* (v23). With this birthright swap, God's promise was coming true!

Full of promise

Isaac

We'll get back to Esau & Jacob in a few days.

But right now we're going to follow their dad, Isaac, around for a bit.

WEIRD WORDS

Famine
Serious lack of food

Philistines
People from the nearby area of Philistia

Oath
Promise

Offspring
Children and descendants

Decrees
Orders

Read Genesis 26 v 1-2

There was a famine and so there was hardly enough food for Isaac and his family. God told Isaac not to go to Egypt for food. God wanted Isaac to stay in the land that He'd promised to give to Isaac's family.

But why should Isaac listen to God?

Read verse 3

God was so good to Isaac! He promised to be with Isaac and to bless Him. And that's not all...

Read verses 4-6

God repeated to Isaac the promises He'd made to Abraham. *To remind yourself of them, go back 1 letter (B=A, C=B, D=C).*

1. Land (v3)

__ ____
J X J M M

_____ ___
H J W F Z P V

___ _____
B M M U I F T F

_____
M B O E T

2. Children (v4)

__ ____
J X J M M

____ ____
N B L F Z P V S

_____
P G G T Q S J O H

__ ____ __
B T N B O Z B T

___ _____
U I F T U B S T

3. Blessing (v4)

__ ____
C Z Z P V S

_____
P G G T Q S J O H

___ _____
B M M O B U J P O T

____ __
X J M M C F

_____
C M F T T F E

What an encouragement! No wonder Isaac obeyed God and stayed away from Egypt! And God is just as loving and faithful to all His children (Christians).

Pray!

Check out some of the promises God made to His people:
Matthew 7 v 7-11
Jeremiah 29 v 11-13
Thank God that He always keeps His promises. Ask Him to help you obey His commands in the Bible.

4

Philistine trouble

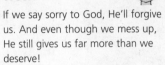

Genesis 26 v 6-22

There's a famine on, so Isaac and Rebekah have gone to the Philistines for food.

WEIRD WORDS

Caressing
Touching

Reaped a hundredfold
Gathered 100 times as many crops as he had planted

Herdsmen
Men who looked after the animals

Esek
Means *dispute*

Sitnah
Means *opposition*

Rehoboth
Means *room*

Read Genesis 26 v 6-11

Isaac was worried that the Philistines would kill him and steal his wife. So he lied, saying that Rebekah was his sister.

It was the same mistake Abraham had made (twice).

King Abimelek had to point out that Isaac was in the wrong.

Think!

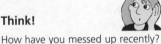

How have you messed up recently? Lied to someone? Been cruel to your brother or sister? Something else?

_____

_____

_____

Tell God about it and say sorry to Him.

Read verses 12-13

Despite Isaac messing up, God still blessed him and made him successful.

Wow!

If we say sorry to God, He'll forgive us. And even though we mess up, He still gives us far more than we deserve!

Speed read verses 14-22

The Philistines were jealous of Isaac's success, so they kept forcing him to move on. But Isaac refused to leave the land God had told him to stay in. So he kept moving around the country until he found the right place.

Read verse 22 again

What did Isaac say?

Pray!

Isaac recognised that God had given him a great place to live. What can YOU thank God for?

_____

_____

_____

Go on then, thank Him!

Peace of the action

Genesis 26 v 23-35

The Philistines were jealous of Isaac's success and kept forcing him to move on from place to place.

WEIRD WORDS

Altar
Table where gifts to God were put

Treaty
Peace agreement

Oath
Serious promise

Shibah
Means *oath*

Beersheba
Means *well of the oath*

Grief
Great sadness

Read Genesis 26 v 23-25

All of today's missing words are in the centre of the page.

The L_____ said to Isaac "Don't be a_____ for I am w_____ you. I will b_____ you and give you many d_____." Isaac built an a_____ to God and worshipped Him.

Isaac had been having a tough time, but he'd be OK because **God was with him**. And when God is with you, awesome things start to happen...

Read verses 26-33

Isaac was visited by King A_____ and his a_____ and army c_____. They had seen that G____ was with I_____! They wanted to make a p_____ agreement with Isaac. Isaac made a f_____ for them and then they agreed their peace treaty.

Think!

Do your friends recognise that God is in your life? Do they see something different about you?

Abimelek adviser afraid altar bless commander descendants Esau feast God Hittites Isaac Lord married peace with wrong

Action!

Here's one way you can show your friends that God is an important part of your life. Slip into conversation that you've been to church / youth group recently. Or mention something exciting you've read in the Bible. Let God become a bigger part of your everyday life.

Read verses 34-35

Isaac's son E_____ made a double mistake.
1) He m_____ two women.
2) Both were H_____ not from God's people.
Both of these things were w_____. More about Esau tomorrow...

Pray!

Dear God, I pray that my friends will see that you're with me and that you're so important to me. May they want to get to know you too.

Disguise surprise

**Genesis
27 v 1-17**

Esau and Jacob
are brothers but
not friends.

Jacob tricked
Esau into giving
up his birthright
(see day 2 for a
reminder).

Now the story
continues...

WEIRD WORDS

Quiver
Pouch for keeping
arrows in

Wild game
Wild animals

Blessing
A special prayer. It
promised important
things for the future.

Read Genesis 27 v 1-4

And cross out the wrong answers.

**Isaac was old/odd and could
no longer sneeze/see. He
told Ezra/Esau/See-saw to
hunt some wild animals and
prepare a tasty eel/meal/
mule for his dad. Then Isaac
would give Esau his blessing/
dressing.**

Isaac's favourite son was Esau.
Rebekah's favourite was Jacob. It
seems that Isaac wanted to bless
Esau in secret so that Rebekah
wouldn't find out.

Read verses 5-10

**Rebekah overheard Isaac
talking to Esau. So she told
Jacob/Esau/Isaac to bring
her two young coats/boats/
goats. She would then cook
the goats for Jacob to take to
Isaac. Isaac would be fooled
into giving his blessing/
bee-sting to Jacob instead of
Esau.**

Read verses 11-13

**Esau was a hairy/furry/fairy
man. Jacob wasn't, and was
worried that Isaac would
touch him and find out the
tooth/truth.**

Jacob was more bothered about
being caught than the fact that
he was lying to his own dad! And
Rebekah didn't seem bothered
about this deception at all!

Read verses 14-17

**Rebekah got Jacob to put
on Esau's bow and arrow/
clothes. She also covered
his hands and nose/neck in
goatskins/suncream. Then
Jacob took the tasty food to
his father.**

Will Jacob and Rebekah get away
with this nasty trick? We'll find out
tomorrow...

Think & pray!

People can be quite persuasive
at times. We have to be on our
guard against being led into
doing stuff that's wrong. Ask
God to give you the strength and
courage to stand up to friends
who want you to do wrong.

Simply the blessed

Genesis 27 v 18-29

Rebekah has persuaded her son Jacob to disguise himself as Esau.

But will Isaac be fooled into blessing Jacob instead of Esau?

Read Genesis 27 v 18-24

How many times did Jacob lie to his father? ☐

He even brought God into his lies (v20)! Shocking!

Have you ever set up a domino chain? You knock over one domino, which flattens the next one, and the next one, and the next one...

Lying can be like that. You tell one lie, and then you have to back it up with another and another...

Think!

Have you been dishonest recently? Spend time saying sorry to God.

Read verses 25-29

Isaac fell for the trick, and blessed Jacob instead of Esau.

Unjumble the anagrams to show how Jacob would be blessed.

1. Great land for growing f_____ and w_____ (v28)
dofo   newi

2. Other nations will s_____ you and bow down to you (v29).
verse

3. You will be lord over your b_____ and they
trobsher
will b_____ d_____ to you (v29).
wob   nowd

4. Those who c_____ you
rescu
will be cursed and those who b_____ you will be
slebs
blessed (v29). (It's part of God's promise to Abraham in Genesis 12 v 3)

No wonder Jacob wanted this blessing! Imagine all of that happening to you.

Now read blessing 3 again. Before Esau and Jacob were born, God told Rebekah...

***"The older will serve the younger"* (Genesis 25 v 23)**

God's plans were coming true! Esau would serve Jacob.

Pray!

Thank God that His plans always work out even when things seem to be going wrong.

Esau is sore

**Genesis
27 v 30-40**

*Jacob fooled Isaac
into giving him
Esau's blessing.
Guess who's
about to get
home...*

WEIRD WORDS

Yoke
Like chains
imprisoning him as a
slave to his brother

Read Genesis 27 v 30-40

The game is up. Isaac found out
too late that he'd been fooled into
blessing his younger son. *How did
he react (v33)?*

*And how did Esau react when he
found out (v34, 38)?*

Esau asked Isaac to bless him too,
but there was no blessing left for
him. Here's what Isaac said to Esau:

Your home will be far from this
land where crops grow so well.
You will stay alive by the power of
your sword and be your brother's
slave. But when you decide to be
free, you will break loose.

Later on in Genesis, we'll read how
all this came true.

No excuse for sin

God had always planned for Jacob
to be more powerful than Esau. But
that doesn't mean Rebekah and
Jacob were right to lie and steal.
It's never right to sin, whatever our
excuse is.

Effects of sin

Look at the rotten effect Jacob's
deception had on the rest of his
family:

**Isaac was furious
Esau was hugely upset
Esau lost everything
Esau wanted to kill Jacob (see
v41)**

Think!

When we live to please ourselves,
we often don't notice how it affects
other people. Is there anyone you
need to apologise to for hurting
them?

The most amazing thing is that
God would still use this family in
His great plans! He would keep His
promises to Abraham, and one day,
Jesus would be born into this family!

Pray!

Thank God that He's always in
control, even when we mess
things up.

Revenge is sour

Jacob has cheated Esau out of the big blessing.

Esau is furious and very upset.

Any ideas what he'll do next?

_____

_____

_____

_____

_____

_____

_____

_____

_____

> **Just you wait till I get hold of you...**

> **I'll get my own back on her**

> **You'll be sorry!**

What word springs to mind? Here's a clue. It starts with an R, has 3 Es in it, a V, N, G and rhymes with Stonehenge. Sort of.

R _ _ _ _ _ _

Got it?

Read Genesis 27 v 41-45

Any feelings of revenge are wrong, but Esau was so angry, that he said he'd k_ _ _ _ J_ _ _ _ _ when Isaac died.

Rebekah heard about this and took swift action:

> **Okay Jacob, you've got to go to your Uncle Laban's place in Harran. Stay there until it's safe to return.**

That's a journey of hundreds of miles! All on his own.

Doing wrong always has bad results, as this family is discovering. *Match up the boxes below by drawing lines between them.*

PERSON	SIN	RESULT
Esau	deceived her husband	made Jacob run for his life
Jacob	wanted to kill his brother	wrecked his father's and brother's lives
Rebekah	deceived his father	lost her favourite son

Think & Pray!

Is there anyone you'd like to get revenge on?

_____

Tell God about it, say sorry to Him, and ask Him to help you to forgive that person.

**Genesis
27 v 46 –
28 v 5**

*Esau wants to kill
Jacob. So it's time
for Jacob to make
a quick exit...*

Run for it!

Read Genesis 27 v 46 – 28 v 2

Unbelievable. Rebekah is still
deceiving her husband! By whining
about Esau's Hittite wives, she
persuades Isaac to send Jacob
away, where he'll be safe from his
murderous brother.

Read verses 3-5

*Use the code to reveal what Isaac
said to Jacob.*

God promised Abraham loads of
descendants and the land of Canaan
for them to live in. These promises
were passed on to Jacob!

Wow!

Jacob was leaving his parents and
starting a new life. The future
looked scary for him. But God was
in control, and would keep His
promises to Jacob. The same is true
for all Christians.

WEIRD WORDS

Hittite women
From Canaan, where
Isaac and his family
lived

Canaanite
Like Hittite

Fruitful
Have lots of children

Aramean
From Aram, an area
hundreds of miles
away

Ishmael
Esau's uncle

Pray!

Thank God that He's in control.
Ask Him to help you when life
seems scary or difficult.

Read verses 6-9 to see Esau mess up again.

A	B	C	D	E	F	G	H	I	K	L	M	N	O	P	R	S	T	U	V	Y

Stairway to heaven

**Genesis
28 v 10-15**

Jacob has left home, and is travelling to his Uncle Laban's home, which is hundreds of miles away.

Time for a rest.

Read Genesis 28 v 10-12

Okay arty-pants, try drawing what Jacob saw in his dream.

The stairway stretching from God to Jacob showed that God was with Jacob all the way.

Read verses 13-14

God repeated His promises to Jacob's family.

1. He'd give them LAND

2. He'd give Jacob loads of DESCENDANTS

3. All nations would be BLESSED by Jacob's family

But God added another promise, just for Jacob. **Read verse 15** *and put it into your own words.*

What an awesome promise for someone who'd let God down several times!

Amazingly, Jacob's dream also reminds us of JESUS, who wouldn't be born for another 1900 years! Look at promise 3 again. Jesus would be born into Jacob's family and would rescue many people from sin!

Check out John 1 v 51

The *Son of Man* means Jesus. When Jesus died and rose again, He became the link (stairway) between God and humans. By trusting in Jesus, we can get to know God. Jesus is the only way to God and eternal life with Him.

Pray!

Thank God that He wants to be with each of us in our lives. Thank Him for sending His Son Jesus to make that possible.

For the free e-booklet
Why Did Jesus Come?, email
discover@thegoodbook.co.uk
or check out
www.thegoodbook.co.uk/contact-us
to find our UK mailing address.

God's house

Genesis 28 v 16-22

Remember what happened to Jacob in yesterday's reading?

Well, I'm not going to remind you, so look it up yourself!

WEIRD WORDS

Pillar
Monument — a place where God would be worshipped

Poured oil on it
To set it apart as a special place for God

Bethel
Means *House of God*

Vow
Promise

How do you think Jacob felt after that amazing dream and those promises from God?

Read Genesis 28 v 16-17

He probably felt all of those things, but he also felt a_____ (v17)

God Himself had been with Jacob all the time, and Jacob had only just realised. It must have been mind-blowing and terrifying!

God had seen everything that Jacob had done, including all his lies and deception. **And God sees everything we do too. Good and bad. Does that freak you out?**

But God had come to bless Jacob, not punish him. **And for us, God sent His Son Jesus. If we turn to Jesus, we can have all our wrongs forgiven, no matter what we've done.**

Read verses 18-19

God had met Jacob there, so he called the place B_____ which means H_____ of G_____.

But Jacob wanted to do more than just leave a stone there. He wanted his whole life to be changed.

Read verses 20-22

Jacob made a promise (vow) to God to say thank you. What was it?

> The L_____ will be my G_____. And I will give Him a t_____ of everything He gives me.

Action!

How about you? How will you show your love to God this week?

_____

_____

_____

Talk to Him about it!

More from Jacob in a few weeks.

Mark: Jesus the King

**Mark
11 v 1-11**

Today we rush to Mark's Gospel to join Jesus on His journey into Jerusalem.

Any guesses what transport he used? (Clue: it's not a Ferrari)

WEIRD WORDS

Bethpage and Bethany
Towns near Jerusalem

Mount of Olives
Large hill near Jerusalem

Colt
Young donkey

The Twelve
Jesus' 12 disciples

WHAT'S GOING ON?

Thousands of people were travelling to Jerusalem to celebrate the most important event of the Jewish year — Passover.

But for Jesus, going to Jerusalem would mean so much more. Check out Mark 10 v 32-34 for the reason.

For Jesus, the road to Jerusalem was also the road to death.

Read Mark 11 v 1-6

Why did Jesus want a donkey???

Check out what the prophet Zechariah said 500 years earlier. **Read Zechariah 9 v 9** *and fill in the missing vowels (aeiou).*

> R__j__ __c__ greatly, Daughter Z__ __n! Sh__ __t, Daughter J__r__s__l__m! See, your k__ng comes to you, righteous and v__ct__rious, l__wly and r__d__ng on a d__nk__y.

Read Mark 11 v 7-11

and see how Zechariah's words came true.

The crowds went wild for King Jesus! *What did they shout (v9)?*

> H__s__nn__!

Wow!

Hosanna means Lord, save us. They were right that Jesus was their King, who had come to save them. But they thought He would save them by fighting the Romans. They didn't realise that Jesus had come to die on the cross to save them from their sins.

A few days later, a crowd would be shouting for Jesus to be killed!

Pray!

Spend time praising Jesus. Thank Him that He came as King to save His people from sin and punishment in hell.

Sing like you mean it!

**Psalm
118 v 19-29**

*Jesus entered
Jerusalem on a
donkey and the
crowds welcomed
Him as their King.*

WEIRD WORDS

The righteous
People who've had
their sins forgiven
by God

Rejoice
Celebrate

Boughs
Tree branches

Festal procession
Procession at a
Jewish festival

Exalt you
Praise and worship
you for your
greatness!

Remember what they shouted to
Him (Mark 11 v 9)?

H_____!

*Bet you can't remember what that
means! Go back 1 letter to find out
(B=A, C=B, D=C).*

Hosanna means _ _ _ _ _
        M P S E

‾ ‾ ‾ ‾   ‾ ‾
T B W F   V T

Read Psalm 118 v 19-29

*Which verse includes the words that
mean Hosanna?*

Verse _____

This psalm was written a long time
before Jesus was born.

Yet it was written about Him.
Decode some of the best bits.

You have become my

_ _ _ _ _ _ _ _
T B M W B U J P O

Salvation means rescue from sin.
Jesus came to save people from the
effects of sin in their lives.

**The stone the builders
rejected has become the**

_ _ _ _ _ _ _ _ _ _
D P S O F S T U P O F

These builders threw away a stone,
not realising it was the *cornerstone*
— the most important stone in the
building!

That's a picture of Jesus.

The people would reject Jesus, not
realising that He was *God's* Son.

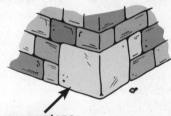

**cornerstone
(the most
important stone
in the building!)**

Think!

Some of the people who were
shouting *Hosanna* now, soon
rejected their King. When you sing
Jesus' praises, do you really mean
what you sing?

Action!

Next time you talk or sing about
Jesus, make sure you check out
the words! Are you being honest
or just pretending?

Figure it out

**Mark
11 v 12-14**

*Josh reckons he's
a Christian.*

*He goes to
church and youth
group, but he
doesn't seem any
different from
his friends who
aren't Christians.*

*It doesn't seem to
have any effect
on him.*

For the free
e-booklet
*How do I know I'm
a Christian?*,
email discover@
thegoodbook.co.uk
or check out
www.thegoodbook.
co.uk/contact-us to
find our UK mailing
address.

Read Mark 11 v 12-14

What a weird story!

*Why do you think Jesus spoke
like that to the tree?*

a) He was starving ☐

b) He hated figs ☐

**c) He was teaching the
disciples something** ☐

The answer is c. So what was Jesus
saying to the disciples?

> **The fig tree looked healthy
> with loads of leaves. Yet, even
> though it looked great, it had
> NO FRUIT.**

> **People in Israel were just like
> this fig tree. They were very
> religious, with a reputation
> for serving God.**

> **They even had God's special
> temple in Jerusalem, to show
> that God was with them.**

> **But underneath, there was no
> real love for God.**
>
> **No real wish to follow Jesus.
> NO FRUIT. One day, the
> temple would be destroyed.
> And Israel would be punished,
> just like the
> fig tree.**

Fig tree

So what's this got to do with us?

Well, we may look good to other
people, we may do religious stuff,
like going to church and not
swearing much... but God sees what
our hearts are really like.

Do we really love God?

Do we obey His Word?

Do we really trust in Jesus?

Do we try to live like Him?

Do we talk to God in prayer?

Action!

Write down ways you can show
fruit in your life. Ways you can
show that you live for God (like
giving Him more of your time,
lying less often etc)

_____

_____

_____

_____

Mark
11 v 15-19

When Jesus got to Jerusalem, He didn't like what He saw...

WEIRD WORDS

Money-changers
They swapped ordinary money for special and expensive temple money, needed to buy gifts for God

Selling doves
For poor people to sacrifice to God

Merchandise
Stuff to sell

Chief priests and teachers of the law
Religious leaders and experts

Turning the tables

Read Mark 11 v 15-17

Jesus was furious! The temple in Jerusalem was the place where God was among His people. *But what did Jesus say they'd turned it into? Unjumble the anagrams.*

A _____
      n e d

of _____
      b e r b o r s

Instead of worshipping God, these guys used the temple to make money and rip people off. They made it expensive to worship — too expensive for some. They were robbing from God too. Robbing Him of the worship He should get in His house.

Think!

Do you rob God of the worship He deserves? Do you thank Him when He answers your prayers? Do you give Him enough of your time? At church, are you focusing on God or other stuff?

What else did Jesus say (v17)?

My temple will be called a

h_____ of
   u s h o e

p_____ for all
   r a y r e p

n_____
   n o s t a i n

Wow!

Jesus would soon die and then be raised back to life. After that, things would change. EVERYONE would be able to get to know God, not just Jewish people.

Double Wow!

And people wouldn't have to go to the temple to meet God anymore. Jesus' death removed the barrier between us and God, so that ANYONE can now meet Him ANYWHERE!

Read verses 18-19

The religious leaders felt threatened by Jesus' popularity, and began to plan His murder.

Pray!

Thank you Jesus, for making it possible for anyone to get to know God personally. Please help me give God the praise and worship He deserves.

⌐

So far, the fruitless fig tree and the incident with the money changers have shown that the temple wasn't all it was cracked up to be.

Today, there's more...

WEIRD WORDS

Rabbi
Teacher

Mountain mover

Read Mark 11 v 20-21

If you can't remember the fig tree, flick back to day 15.

Read verses 22-23

So what's all this mountain stuff?

> ### Mountain stuff
> When Jesus said "this mountain", He was referring to Mount Zion, in Jerusalem, with the temple on top.

Until now, to meet God, everyone had to go to the temple on the mountain in Jerusalem. But remember, the cursed fig tree showed that God would punish the Israelites and destroy the temple.

What??? No temple? How can we meet God? That's how we've always met God!

Fill in the vowels (aeiou) to reveal Jesus' answer (it's in v22).

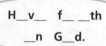

H__v__ f__ __th __n G__d.

That means **trust God**.
He can sort the problem out!

Wow!

Through Jesus, God was going to change things so ANYONE ANYWHERE could pray to Him. You wouldn't need to go to the temple. So it wouldn't matter if the temple jumped into the sea!

Read verses 24-25

and complete these two top tips for praying.

1. B___l___ ___v___ that God can do what you ask (v24).

2. F___rg___v___ people you're angry with (v25).

Pray!

Thank God that through Jesus you can pray anytime, anywhere, for anything that's right and good. So get praying right now!

Tricky questions

As usual, the
religious leaders
are up to no
good.

They want Jesus'
blood and they're
out to trap Him.

Read on...

WEIRD WORDS

Elders
Jewish leaders

Baptism
John dunked people
in water to show
that they had turned
away from sin and
now lived for God

Prophet
God's messenger

Read Mark 11 v 27-28
Decode their trick question.

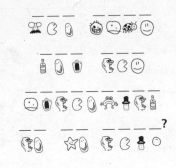

In other words: *"What gives you
the right to kick people out of the
temple?"* (see day 16). Jesus had to
be careful...

> If He said: **"God gives me
> this authority"**, they could
> arrest Him for blasphemy
> (telling lies about God) and
> sentence Him to death.

> And if Jesus said: **"No one
> has given me authority to
> do this"**, He'd be shown
> up to be a big fraud.

So Jesus asked
them His own trick
question...

**Read verses
29-33**

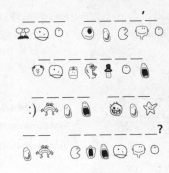

John the Baptist told people to get
ready for Jesus, God's promised
King. So the question is: Did John's
message about Jesus come from
God or not?

> If they said that John's
> message came from God,
> they'd be admitting that
> Jesus came from God too!

> But if they said it wasn't
> from God, they feared the
> crowds would turn
> against them.

So they refused to answer the
question. And so did Jesus.

Think!

Who do YOU think Jesus is? Just
a man, or God's Son, who came
to rescue you?

A B C D E F G H I J M N O P R S T U V W Y

Vine sign

Q: What's the difference between a parrot, a parable and a parachute?

A: Jesus only used one of them to teach us stuff!

Read Mark 12 v 1-8

Like all of Jesus' parables, this is a picture to teach us something. Here's what it means...

Who's who?

Vineyard owner = God

Vineyard = God's people, the Israelites (Jews)

Tenants = Jewish leaders

Servants = God's messengers (prophets)

Verse 1

The vineyard is a picture of God's people. He gave them His laws to keep, and appointed leaders to rule His people.

The owner wanted fruit from the vineyard. This is like God looking for *fruit* from His people — expecting them to love and obey Him.

Verse 2

So who did God send?

A s_____

In the Old Testament, God sent His servants (prophets, like Elijah) to tell His people to start obeying Him again.

Verses 3-5

How were the servants treated?

_____

_____

This is how God's prophets were treated. They were mocked, ignored or killed.

Verses 6-8

Who did the vineyard owner eventually send?

His s_____

What happened to him?

_____

_____

God sent His only Son, Jesus, to the Israelites. Did they listen to Him?
YES/NO _____

They wanted Him dead!

Pray!

People today still mock or ignore Jesus. What about you? God sent Jesus to us, knowing He would die for our sin. Tell God how that makes you feel.

Tomorrow: the story continues...

WEIRD WORDS

Vineyard
Where grapes for wine are grown

Winepress
Where grapes are crushed to make wine

Tenants
People who rented the vineyard from the owner

A big mistake?

**Mark
12 v 9-12**

*Recap: Jesus
is telling us a
parable about a
guy who rented
out his vineyard.*

*But when he
sent servants to
collect fruit from
the vineyard,
the tenants beat
up some and
murdered others.*

*Even the owner's
son was killed.*

How would you feel if you were the vineyard owner?

Read Mark 12 v 9

The owner was very angry.
Unjumble the anagrams, please.

The tenants will be

k_____
l e d l i k

The vineyard will be given

to · o_____
s h e r o t

This parable is about the religious leaders. They refused to believe that Jesus was God's promised King. So they decided to kill Him! But they made a **BIG MISTAKE** about Jesus...

Read verses 10-12

Remember reading about this important stone in Psalm 118 (back on day 14)?

The s_____ the
n o t e s

builders r_____
j e t c r e e d

has become the

c_____
n e r r o c n o t e s

the most important stone
of all!

This is all about Jesus. The religious leaders had made a **BIG MISTAKE** about Jesus. He was the most important person they would ever meet. He was the King who God sent to rescue His people. Yet the religious leaders arrested Him, beat Him, and crucified Him.

Wow!

But it wasn't all a mistake! Jesus had already told His disciples that He had come to die. It was all part of God's plan!

Need a reminder?

Look up **Romans 5 v 8** and write it out on a sheet of paper. You could even turn it into a poster and stick it up on your wall.

Pray!

Thank God for sending His Son, Jesus, to die for His people, and rescue them from sin.

Tax debate

Mark 12 v 13-17

Q – A train travelling from Newcastle, and a train travelling from Brighton crash exactly halfway. Where are the survivors buried?

_____

_____

A – The SURVIVORS aren't buried anywhere. They're still alive!

Sorry, that was a devious trick question! Jesus' enemies (the Pharisees and Herodians) liked trick questions too. But they wanted to trick Jesus into trouble.

Read Mark 12 v 13-15

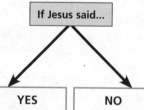

Should we pay taxes to Caesar and the Romans, or not?

If Jesus said...

YES	**NO**
They could accuse Him of siding with the Romans against the Jews.	They could accuse Him of breaking Roman tax laws.

What did Jesus say?

Read verses 16-17

Give Emperor Caesar what _____

_____

It's right to pay taxes and obey the government's laws. But also,

Give God what

_____

_____

God created us, so we should give our lives to Him, obeying and serving Him.

Think!

Today, how can you give to God what belongs to Him?

Spending time with Him
Thanking Him   Loving others
Doing what the Bible teaches
Loving Him   Praising Him

Now talk to God about it...

Acts: Spread the news

**Acts
1 v 1-8**

The book of Acts was written by Luke (the same man who wrote Luke's Gospel).

Acts is all about how Jesus' disciples (now called apostles) began to spread the gospel. The **GOSPEL** is the good news that Jesus died for us and was raised back to life.

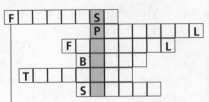

Read Acts 1 v 1-8

Before Jesus went back to heaven to rule as King, He gave the apostles His final instructions.

They were sent to tell the world that Jesus had come back to life and beaten death. This message would make many people hate them. But Jesus was going to give them the power to do it.

POWERFUL	STRONG
UNBELIEVING	FRIGHTENED
TRUSTING	LOST HOPE
RAN AWAY	FAITHFUL
FEARLESS	BRAVE

From the word pool, find the words which describe the apostles when Jesus was crucified (clue in Mark 14 v 50).

Who could possibly have brought about this dramatic change in the disciples? The shaded letters tell us...

Jesus was going to send them His Holy Spirit. Read verse 8.

Then they would have the power they needed to spread the good news to the world.

WEIRD WORDS

Theophilus
Man who Luke wrote to about Jesus

Holy Spirit
He helps all Christians to serve God

Apostles
Men who God sent to tell people about Jesus

Baptised
Dunked people in water as a sign of turning to God

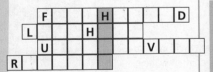

*The other words in the pool describe what the apostles were like **afterwards**. Fit them into the second grid.*

Pray!

The Holy Spirit isn't a force like electricity, but a person. He's God! On their own, the apostles were pretty ordinary. But with God's help, they could tell everyone about Jesus. And so can we! Ask for God's help. Ask God to help you even when it seems hard.

23

Acts
1 v 9-11

Jesus told the apostles to go and tell the world about Him.

And He would give them the Holy Spirit to help them.

But now it's time for Jesus to leave...

Global warning

Read Acts 1 v 9

After Jesus had been raised back to life, He spent 40 days with His followers, teaching them loads. Then He went back to heaven to be with His Father.

Read verses 10-11

Maybe the apostles gazed up for a long time, hoping that Jesus would come back.

What did the two angels say to the apostles? Take the words from the first speech bubble and put them in the correct order in the second speech bubble.

sky? do the
looking you Why
stand into here

It's true that Jesus **will** come back. But there's no point in waiting around doing nothing until He does! Before then, the apostles (and all Christians) have a great task to do.

*Complete what Jesus said in **Acts 1 v 8**, by writing around the world.*

You will be my witnesses in Jerusalem, Judea, Samaria and

That was the great task that Jesus gave the apostles. And it's still being carried out now, by Christians all around the world. Only when the work is complete will Jesus come back.

Think!

In the meantime, are you carrying out Jesus' great task? Are you telling people about Him and how He can forgive all our sins? It's a tough task, but God will help us to do it.

Pray!

Ask God to give you the courage to tell people about Jesus and what He achieved by dying on the cross and being raised back to life.

Acts
1 v 12-19

Don't pretend

Jesus has left His followers and gone back to heaven. How will these guys cope without Him?

Read Acts 1 v 12-14

What did these believers do regularly (v14)?

P_____

Action!

It's important for believers to meet together to pray. Who can YOU meet up with to pray together?

_____

_____

_____

_____

Read verses 15-19

Do you remember how Judas handed Jesus over to His enemies? Judas had seemed to be Jesus' friend and follower but he betrayed Jesus.

Sadly, there are many people like Judas today. People who say they are Christians but don't really love Jesus.

Think!

What about you? It's easy to go to church or youth group and act like you're a Christian. But do you actually love Jesus?

Judas deeply regretted what he'd done. But he didn't turn away from his wrong ways. Or ask God to forgive him. He committed suicide (it's in Matthew 27 v 5).

Wow!

But there's good news for us! Jesus wants to forgive all our sins! There's no need for anyone to choose hell instead. Have YOU asked Jesus to forgive your sins?

If you want to know more about becoming a Christian, email discover@thegoodbook.co.uk or check out www.thegoodbook.co.uk/contact-us to find our UK mailing address.

WEIRD WORDS

Sabbaths day's walk
About 1,100 metres. Jews were not allowed to walk further on a Sabbath.

Believers
People who believed that Jesus was God's Son

Scripture
Old Testament

Fulfilled
Come true

David
King David who fought Goliath, & wrote psalms

Ministry
God's work

**Acts
1 v 20-26**

Yesterday we read the tragic tale of Judas and how he betrayed Jesus.

Apostle appointment

Judas had gone, so another man was needed to take his place. They knew it was right to replace him, because the event had been predicted 1000 years earlier!

Read Acts 1 v 20-23

Who should they choose? Well, whoever they choose must have the right qualities for the great work of spreading the gospel.

Find the missing words in the verses. Then decode the qualities needed for the job.

He must be one of the

m_ _ **who was with them**
  1

all the _ _ _ _ **that the**
    2 3 4 5

L_ _ _ **Jesus was there**
 6

(v21)

Quality 1

C_ _ _ _ _ _ _ _ _ _
 6 4 4 3 2 4 5 1 2

He could be a reliable witness. Christians should tell people the truth about Jesus too.

Read verses 24-26

They p_ _ _ _ _ _
        7 8

asking God which of these

t_ _ **men God had**
 9

_ _osen. **They cast lots**
10 11

(threw dice) and

M_ _ _ _ _ _ _
        12 13

was chosen.

Quality 2

G_ _ ' _ _ _ _ _ _ _ _
 9 8 13 10 11 9 12 10 7

Most importantly, the person serving God must be the person **God** wants for the job! God uses different people to serve Him in different ways.

Wow!

If you are a Christian, God has already chosen you to serve Him! He calls all believers to live for Him and tell others about Jesus.

Pray!

Ask God to show you how you can serve Him. Ask Him to give you the courage to live for Him, telling people about Jesus.

WEIRD WORDS

Dwell
Live

John's baptism
When John the Baptist baptised Jesus

Resurrection
Being raised back to life

Apostolic ministry
Telling people about Jesus!

Great **tongues** of fire

**Acts
2 v 1-13**

*1000s of people
from many
countries went
to Jerusalem
to celebrate
the feast of
Pentecost.*

WEIRD WORDS

Pentecost
Special feast to thank
God for the harvest

Other tongues
Languages

God-fearing
Obeyed God

Bewilderment
Confusion

Galileans
Men from Galilee, in
the north of Israel

Perplexed
Baffled

*Go back one letter (B=A, C=B etc)
to show some of the places people
travelled from.*

```
_ _ _ _ _
J U B M Z
```

```
_ _ _ _ _
U V S L F Z
```

```
_ _ _ _ _
D S F U F
```

```
_ _ _ _ _
F H Z Q U
```

Read Acts 2 v 1-4

*Draw or write the three strange
things that happened.*

Verse 2:

Verse 3:

Verse 4:

Jesus gave the apostles the **Holy
Spirit** to help them tell people
about Him. The Holy Spirit helped
the apostles to speak in many
languages! Why?

Read verses 5-13

Look back at the map. Those are
just some of the many different
places people came from to
celebrate Pentecost in Jerusalem.
God gave the apostles the ability to
tell all these people about Him in
their own languages!

Wow!

God wants the **WHOLE WORLD** to
know about Jesus! And God wants
us to tell people about Jesus too.

That might mean talking to people
from different parts of the world, or
the person living next door!

Pray!

Do you know any Christians in
other countries?

_____

_____

_____

_____

Pray for them right now, asking
God to help them tell people
about Jesus. Pray the same for
yourself too!

That's the Spirit!

Peter explained what was really going on. It had all been predicted 800 years earlier by the prophet Joel.

Read Acts 2 v 14-18

Joel had said that God's Spirit would come in a dramatic way.

Fill in the gaps please!

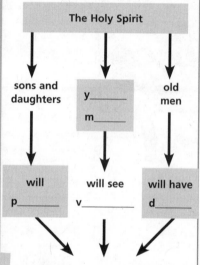

The Holy Spirit

| sons and daughters | y_____ m_____ | old men |

| will p_____ | will see v_____ | will have d_____ |

Exciting stuff! The Holy Spirit enabled these ordinary people to do extraordinary things for God. It doesn't always happen with visions and dreams. But God does give His Spirit to all believers, helping them to serve Him, understand the Bible and tell people about Jesus!

There will be other demonstrations of God's power before Jesus returns at the end of the world.

Read verses 19-21

The Holy Spirit helped the apostles tell people about Jesus in loads of different languages!

Some people thought the apostles were drunk, but Peter put them straight...

WEIRD WORDS

The Eleven
The rest of the apostles

Jews
God's people, the Israelites

Prophesy
Tell people God's message

Sounds terrifying. But we shouldn't worry too much about these things or exactly when Jesus will return. The most important thing is in **verse 21**. *Write it out below.*

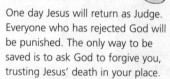

Wow!

One day Jesus will return as Judge. Everyone who has rejected God will be punished. The only way to be saved is to ask God to forgive you, trusting Jesus' death in your place.

Pray!

Have you turned to God to be saved and forgiven?
Talk to God about it and how it makes you feel.

Peter is talking to a large crowd all about Jesus.

Let's listen in...

WEIRD WORDS

Accredited by God
God proved that Jesus was His Son, the Christ

Foreknowledge
It was all part of God's plan

My tongue rejoices
I'm loudly happy!

Holy One
Jesus

Patriarch
Famous ancestor

Messiah
The Rescuer

Peter pipes up

Read Acts 2 v 22-24

Peter mentioned three things.

1. Jesus' life

The amazing things Jesus did and said, proving that He was God's Son.

2. Jesus' death

It was God's plan for Jesus to die to take the punishment we deserve.

3. Jesus' resurrection

God raised Jesus back to life. Jesus beat death and sin and is now King in heaven!

Action!

That's easy to remember! Spend time memorising those three things. It will help you to tell your friends about Jesus.

Read verses 25-28

King David said this 1000 years before Peter was speaking. So what's it got to do with Jesus?

Read verse 29

Peter is saying that David is dead and buried. So this stuff can't be about David, because it was saying this person would be raised from the dead. So it must be about someone else!

Read verses 30-31

David knew Jesus would be his descendant. The psalm is written as though it is Jesus speaking to His Father God.

Read verses 25-28 again

Write the correct verse numbers after each explanation of what it means.

Jesus was supported by His Father, so He wouldn't be **SHAKEN** from His purpose of dying for sinners like you and me.

Verse _____

God wouldn't leave Jesus' body in the **GRAVE** to **DECAY**.

Verse _____

Jesus knew the way to everlasting **LIFE** in heaven. He would be full of **JOY** when He saw His Father there.

Verse _____

Pray!

We've learned loads about Jesus today. So I'll let you decide what you want to praise and thank God for.

The Man who matters

**Acts
2 v 32-36**

Peter is telling a huge crowd that Jesus really was God's Son and He really was raised back to life.

WEIRD WORDS

Exalted
Raised up to an important position

Ascend
Go up

Be assured
Be confident. Know that it's true.

Crucified
Nailed to a cross and left to die

Messiah
The Rescuer

Find a home for each of these words somewhere on the page.

Holy   raised   sent
Messiah   hand   Spirit
right   crucified   Lord

Read Acts 2 v 32-33
Complete what Peter said.

Jesus lived, died and rose again, just as the Old Testament said He would. Now He is r_____ to the r_____ h_____ of God — He is in heaven. And the amazing miracles you have just seen are because God s_____ His H_____ S_____ as He promised!

On Day 23 we read about Jesus going back up to heaven. That had been predicted in the Old Testament too!

Read verses 34-35
What was David saying?

The Lord
(God the Father)
                ...said to my Lord
                              (Jesus)
...sit at my right hand
(Jesus went back to heaven to rule with His Father)

The stuff Peter's been quoting from the Old Testament has been hard to follow. But his conclusion is very clear...

Read verse 36

God has made Jesus both L_____ (the one you should serve) and M_____ (the one God promised would come to save you) ... and you c_____d Him!

What a terrible thing to have done. Tomorrow we'll see how the people react to Peter's hard words. In the meantime...

Pray!

The Old Testament shows us that God promised to send Jesus to rescue people. Thank God for keeping His promise.
And thank God that Jesus is now in heaven, ruling as King of everything.

Heart pains

Acts
2 v 37-40

Peter has told the crowd that Jesus came to rescue them and that they are responsible for His death.

Let's see how they reacted to these hard words...

WEIRD WORDS

Baptised
Washed in water as a sign of turning away from sin and turning to God

Corrupt generation
All the people who refused to live God's way

Read Acts 2 v 37

When these people realised what they had done to Jesus, it hurt them like a knife wound.

Think!

When you think about the times you've let Jesus down, does it hurt you? If it does, say sorry to Him right now.

The people couldn't bear the pain any longer. *Fill in their big question (v37).*

Read verse 38

What was Peter's first word?

R_____

That means turn away from your sins and turn to Jesus.

That was the only way they could get rid of the hurt. They must turn **away** from their wrong ways (sin) and turn **towards** Jesus.

To everyone who does turn away from their wrong ways, there's a brilliant double promise...

Read verse 38 again

and complete the promises.

1. Your s_____ will be forgiven!
Trusting Jesus to rescue you and turning away from your sinful ways means God will forgive you!

2. You will r_____ the gift of the H_____ S_____
To everyone who turns to Jesus and becomes a Christian, God gives the Holy Spirit, helping them to live God's way!

Read verses 39-40

ANYONE who God calls can turn to Jesus for forgiveness!

Pray!

To repent doesn't just mean saying sorry. It means asking God to help you to **CHANGE** and live for Him. Do you want God to help you to change?
If so, tell Him now.

**Acts
2 v 41-47**

Peter has been telling a large crowd all about Jesus.

3000 of them want to turn away from their sinful ways and live for Jesus!

WEIRD WORDS

Fellowship
Christians spending time together, supporting each other and growing together

Awe
Amazement

Sincere hearts
They really were happy to be living God's way!

New start

What next?

Read Acts 2 v 41

They all got baptised.

That must have taken aaaages!

Baptism – the facts

- Getting baptised means being washed in water to show that you follow Jesus.

- Being **baptised** is being washed on the **outside**.

- Being **forgiven** by God is like being washed on the **inside**.

- Baptism is an **outside** sign of an **inside** change.

Read verses 42-47

daerb   deen

seltsopa

desiarp   deyarp

Use the backwards word pool to reveal what these new Christians did.

1. They learned from the a_____' teaching (v42)

We should listen to people who tell us about the Bible.

2. They broke b_____ together (v42)

Christians eat the communion (or the Lord's Supper) meal together. It reminds them of Jesus' death for them.

3. They p_____ (v42)

It's important for Christians to talk to God in prayer – on our own and with other Christians.

4. They sold their possessions and gave to people in n_____ (v45)

Christians should share what they have, and look after people who are in need.

5. P_____ God (v47)

Christians praise and thank God together for all that He has done for them.

Think & pray!

Which of those five things do you really need to do more?

_____

_____

Ask God to help you give more of your life to serving Him.

Philippians: Shine!

**Philippians
2 v 12-18**

*Want to live
God's way? Paul
gives us some
great advice...*

WEIRD WORDS

Salvation
Rescue from sin

**Warped/
crooked**
Very sinful

Day of Christ
When Jesus returns
as King

Labour
Work

**Drink offering/
sacrifice**
Liquid poured out
as a sacrifice to
God. Paul's life was
being given to serve
God.

Read Philippians 2 v 12-13

> God has rescued you
> from sin, so keep living
> His way, pleasing Him.
> God works in your lives to
> make it possible for you
> to serve Him!

Read verses 14-16

*Fill in the missing vowels (aeiou) to
reveal Paul's top tips for living God's
way.*

1. Do __v__ryth__ng
w__th__ __t gr__mbl__ng
or __rg__ __ng (v14)

Don't moan about serving God —
it's a great privilege!

And cut out arguing with other
Christians; it only slows down God's
work.

2. Sh__n__ l__k__ st__rs in
the sky (v15)

Christians should try to cut out sin
from their lives. We live in a world
that is full of sin. We must live lives
that shine out in a dark world.
People should see how great it is to
serve Jesus.

3. H__ld f__rmly to the
w__rd of l__f__ (v16)

The word of life is the gospel —
the great news that Jesus can
give people everlasting life. It's a
message we need to hold on firmly
to ourselves, and also to be telling
people!

Read verses 17-18

> Even as I'm facing
> execution for spreading
> the gospel, I'm still happy
> that you're living God's
> way and telling people
> about Jesus.

Action!

Read through the 3 boxes of Paul's
advice. Which one do you need to
do something about?

_____

What will you do about it?

_____

_____

_____

Pray!

Thank God that He works in your
life to make you more like Jesus.
Ask His help with what you've
decided to do.

Top man Tim

Philippians 2 v 19-24

Are you out-going, energetic, a born leader?

Or quiet, shy and reserved?

How would you describe yourself?

_____

_____

_____

_____

_____

WEIRD WORDS

Welfare
Happiness and well-being. How they're getting along.

Read Philippians 2 v 19-24

Paul wanted to send Timothy to visit the Christians in Philippi. Paul and Timothy were very different types of people...

Paul

**An old man.
He was Jewish.
An experienced leader.**

Timothy

**A young man.
A Gentile (not a Jew).
Just starting out as a leader.**

Yet there was a very special friendship between Paul and Timothy.

Like a s_____ with his

f_____ (v22)

What made these very different men such close friends?

Go forward two letters to find out (A=C, B=D, C=E etc).

He has

$\overline{~}$ $\overline{~}$ $\overline{~}$ $\overline{~}$ $\overline{~}$ $\overline{~}$
Q C P T C B

$\overline{~}$ $\overline{~}$ $\overline{~}$ $\overline{~}$ $\overline{~}$ $\overline{~}$ $\overline{~}$ $\overline{~}$
U G R F   K C   G L

$\overline{~}$ $\overline{~}$ $\overline{~}$ $\overline{~}$ $\overline{~}$ $\overline{~}$ $\overline{~}$
R F C   U M P I

$\overline{~}$ $\overline{~}$ $\overline{~}$ $\overline{~}$ $\overline{~}$
M D   R F C

$\overline{~}$ $\overline{~}$ $\overline{~}$ $\overline{~}$ $\overline{~}$ (v22)
E M Q N C J

It's the **gospel**, the good news about Jesus, that's behind their friendship. The great truth about Jesus brings together people of different backgrounds, nationalities and personalities.

Both Paul and Timothy...

• **cared deeply about sharing the gospel.**

• **cared for their Christian friends.**

• **were glad to be servants of Jesus Christ.**

• **went out of their way to serve others.**

Pray!

Whatever kind of person you are, God can use you to serve Him! Ask God to make you more like Paul and Timothy. Especially in those four ways above.

Oh brother!

Philippians 2 v 25-30

Epaphroditus

Yesterday Paul told us about his friend Timothy.

Today we meet another top man.

WEIRD WORDS

Fellow soldier
Fighting on God's side, against sin

Had mercy on him
God showed him great kindness and healed him

Anxiety
Worry

Your mate George is in hospital with his leg in plaster, and he asks you...

> Could you do me a huge favour and deliver this parcel? Sorry, but it's a few miles out of your way.

What would you say?

> Can't someone else go?

> Er, sorry, I'm really busy!

> No problem, I'll go now.

The Philippian Christians had sent Epaphroditus to visit Paul and look after him. He was prepared to travel 100s of miles for Paul and for the gospel!

Read Philippians 2 v 25-30

Epaphroditus almost died. It must have been tough, but he knew that in helping Paul he was also working for Christ.

Read verse 26 again

He didn't even think about himself! Top man. No wonder Paul spoke so highly of him.

Unjumble the anagrams to reveal some of the things Paul called Epaphroditus.

B_____
HERTROB

CO-W_____
ROWREK

F_____ S_____
WOLFEL OLDRISE

Do you know anyone like Epaphroditus? Someone who will do anything to serve Jesus?

Action!

Paul tells us how we should treat them in verse 29.

Welcome them   Value them

Honour them   Respect them

GO ON, TRY IT YOURSELF!

Pray!

Thank God for the person you wrote down. Ask Him to help you to be a friend to them and to encourage them.

**Philippians
3 v 1-6**

Beware of the dogs!

Back to Paul's letter to the Christians in Philippi.

Read Philippians 3 v 1-2

False teachers had told the Philippians lies. They said that to be a Christian you had to be circumcised. It wasn't true. Paul called them dogs and said they were evil for saying such things.

Circumcision

Old Testament laws said that all male Israelites had to have part of the skin around their penis cut off. It was a sign that they belonged to God.

But when **JESUS** came, He made it possible for **anyone** (not just Israelites) to become part of God's people. So circumcision is no longer necessary.

Read verse 3

Paul is saying that Christians are God's true people. Being circumcised is no longer a sign of belonging to God, but these three things are...

1. Serving God

Serving God and living our lives for Him. The Holy Spirit helps Christians to do this.

2. Boasting in Jesus Christ

Christians are so happy that they know Jesus and that He has rescued them from sin.

3. Not trusting in ourselves

Nothing we can do can put us right with God. Going to church, living a good life, getting circumcised... none of it is good enough.

Think!

Read through those three signs of being a Christian. Are they true of you?

Read verses 4-6

Before he was a Christian, Paul was a Jewish leader. Fill in the missing letters of his description.

**Paul was an Israe__ite from
the tribe of B__njamin, a top
Hebr__w.
He was circ__mcised when
he was 8 days old. He was a
Phari__ee, he kept Jewi__h
law and he per__ecuted
Christians.**

(missing letter numbers: Israe_4_ite, B_5_njamin, Hebr_3_w, circ_1_mcised, Phari_6_ee, Jewi_2_h, per_7_ecuted)

Put the missing letters in order.

All these things were

$\overline{\quad}_1 \overline{\quad}_2 \overline{\quad}_3 \overline{\quad}_4 \overline{\quad}_5 \overline{\quad}_6 \overline{\quad}_7$

**when it came to
pleasing God.**

Living a good life isn't enough to get right with God and have our sins forgiven. Tomorrow, we'll discover the only way to get right with God.

WEIRD WORDS

Rejoice
Celebrate

Safeguard
Helpful reminder

Mutilators of the flesh
They circumcised people for the wrong reasons

Boast in Christ
Are proud to know Jesus

Hebrews
Israelites, God's special people

Zeal
Enthusiasm

Righteousness based on the law
Feeling good for keeping the law

What a load of garbage!

**Philippians
3 v 7-11**

*Look back at
the end of
yesterday's page
to see what Paul
was like before
he became a
Christian.*

WEIRD WORDS

**Surpassing
worth**
Bigger value

Righteousness
Being right
with God

The law
Old Testament
commands

Faith
Belief, trust

Resurrection
Being raised back
to life

GARBAGE!

That's what Paul now thought of
all those things he used to be so
proud of.

Read Philippians 3 v 7-11

Many people today are proud
of their lives. They feel sure they
live good enough lives to make
themselves right with God.

> I try to do my best.

> I go to church
> every Sunday.

> I give loads of
> money away.

**OK, so these are all good
things. But on their own
they're nowhere near good
enough to satisfy God.
Not enough to receive
eternal life. It's like offering
God garbage and expecting
Him to be pleased!**

Paul knew what was **garbage** in his
life and he was willing to throw it all
away so that he could grasp the real
treasure — **KNOWING JESUS.**

Read verse 8 again; *then write out
its amazing words on spare paper.
You could make a poster.*

Paul knew that only *"Christ's
righteousness"* (His perfect life,
and death on the cross) could make
Paul pleasing to God. How?

**through f_____h
in Jesus Christ (v9)**

Wow!

Only Jesus dying in our place
can make us right with God.
Only trusting Him to forgive our sins
will give us eternal life with Him.

Pray!

Want to please God and have
your sins forgiven by Him? Then
tell Him and ask Him right now!
Then talk to an older Christian
about it.

Want to know how to become a
Christian? For the free e-booklet
What's it all about?, email
discover@thegoodbook.co.uk
or check out
www.thegoodbook.co.uk/contact-us
to find our UK mailing address.

On the run

37

**Philippians
3 v 12-16**

*Christine has
been training for
years and now
she's finally at the
Olympics!*

*But she's not
satisfied with just
running in the
race.*

*She wants the
prize — she wants
to win.*

WEIRD WORDS

Obtained
Got

Mature
People who had
grown as Christians

Attained
Achieved

Paul says that Christians are like athletes, and the prize they're running for is **eternal life** with God! But some of the Christians in Philippi had stopped putting effort into living for God. They were happy with the way things were.

Read Philippians 3 v 12-14

Use the word blocks to complete what Paul is saying.

Christ	**press**	**Jesus**
prize	**Christ**	**Jesus**
goal	**God**	**perfect**

**I haven't already been made
p_____.
But I p_____ on to
take hold of that which
C_____ J_____
took hold of for me. I press
on towards the g_____
to win the p_____ for
which G_____ has called me
heavenwards in
C_____ J_____.**

Who is at the centre of Paul's race and Paul's life?

C_____ J_____

Paul knew he wasn't perfect. He could still become more godly and do so much more to serve God.

Wow!

Don't get lazy! There's still so much more we can do for God! More people to tell about Jesus. More sins to conquer. More of the Bible to read. More ways we can serve God. Don't stop running for God!

Read verses 15-16

Double wow!

Christians have had their sins forgiven by Jesus Christ. And they should live in a way that is pleasing to Him.

Pray!

Ask God to help you keep living His way, serving Him more and more. Ask Him to correct you and teach you more about pleasing Him.

At home in heaven

**Philippians
3 v 17–4 v 1**

*What country
does/will your
passport have
on it?*

_____

*That makes you
a CITIZEN of
that country.*

WEIRD WORDS

Destiny
What will definitely
happen to them

Saviour
Rescuer

Lowly bodies
Weak bodies that
get ill and die

Joy and crown
Paul loves them and
is proud of them

Today Paul tells us about 2 kinds of
people. People who **hate** Jesus and
people who **love** Him. Citizens of
earth and citizens of **heaven**.

Read Philippians 3 v 17-19

Paul is so upset by these people that
he's in tears as he writes!

Why? Go back 1 letter to find out.

They were

___ ___ ___ ___ ___ ___   ___ ___
f o f n j f t   p g

___ ___ ___   ___ ___ ___ ___ ___
u i f   d s p t t

> **Verse 19 tells us what
> these people were like:**
> - **heading to hell, not
>   heaven**
> - **boasting about their sin,
>   not about Jesus**
> - **more concerned with
>   other things than with
>   serving God**

That's true of anyone who chooses
to live their own way instead of
God's. They are **enemies of Jesus**.

So how are Christians different?

Read verses 20-21

1. Christians are citizens of

___ ___ ___ ___ ___ ___ **(v20)**
i f b w f o

That's where they belong, and one
day they'll live there with Jesus!
Christians should be more bothered
about serving Jesus than earthly
stuff like possessions.

2. Christians can't wait for

___ ___ ___ ___ ___ **to come again**
K f t v t

They'll get to be with Jesus for ever.
And He will give them brand new
bodies that won't get ill or die!

Read Philippians 4 v 1

3. Christians should

___ ___ ___ ___ ___   ___ ___ ___ ___
t u b o e   g j s n

in their belief that Jesus has died
for them and will give them
everlasting life.

Pray!

Do you know anyone who refuses
to live God's way?
Ask the Lord to transform their
lives so that they switch from
being enemies of Jesus to being
His friends.

**Philippians
4 v 2-3**

Sort it out!

Read Philippians 4 v 2

Paul wants to help sort out a disagreement between two women at the church in Philippi.

Who were they?

E_____ and

S_____

Have you ever tried sorting out a big argument?

Maybe between two of your friends?

It's not easy, is it?! And it often seems to make things worse.

Paul valued these two women. Both of them were Christians who had helped Paul **"in the cause of the gospel"(v3).**

Paul was really tactful. He knew it didn't matter whose fault it was — the important thing was to sort out the argument.

Paul's advice to them is relevant to us too. Find it by crossing out all the Xs, Ys and Zs, then following the maze.

Wow!

When Christians fall out, they need to remember that they both serve God. Any disagreements should be sorted out so they can get back to serving God together.

Read verse 3

Paul also asked other Christians in the church to help these two sort out their problems.

Think!

Got any Christian friends who have fallen out?

_____

```
Z G R E E Z Z
  A Y X W X Y
X Z X Y I Y D
Y Z E H T Z R
H C A Z Y X O
O X X Z X Z L
T H Y N T H E
Z E R I X Y Z
```

A_ _ _ _ _   _ _ _ _ _

_ _ _ _ _   _ _ _ _ _

_ _ _ _   _ _ _ _ _

WEIRD WORDS

True companion
Probably a leader in the church

Contended
Helped Paul tell people about Jesus

Book of life
It means they're Christians

Pray!

Ask God to help your friends sort things out. Ask Him to show you how you can gently help them become friends. And if you've fallen out with anyone, ask God to help you say sorry and sort that out too.

Philippians 4 v 4-7

Paul's got some great advice for the Christians in Philippi.

And it's great advice for anyone who wants to live for God.

WEIRD WORDS

Evident
Obvious

Anxious
Worried

Petition
Asking God for things

Transcends understanding
Is more than we can understand

Trio of top tips

Read the verses and fill in the vowels to complete Paul's advice.

Read Philippians 4 v 4

1. R__j__ __c__ in the L__rd

What does that mean? Grin stupidly? Go around shouting *"HALLELUJAH"*? Nope. It means we should be **excited** about God and what He's done for us, even when we're feeling low. That's rejoicing.

How often? __lw__ys

Read verse 5

2. Be g__ntl__

We should be considerate to other people. If Christians show people kindness and consideration, they will notice and want to know why. It's just part of living God's way.

Read verse 6

3. Don't w__rry about __nyth__ng but take your r__q__ __sts to G__d with th__nksg__v__ng

You don't need to worry so much! Take your problems to God when your pray. Tell Him all about them and ask Him to sort them out. And **thank** Him for how great He is!

The Result?
Read verse 7

The p__ __c__ of G__d will guard your h__ __rts and m__nds in Chr__st J__s__s

God looks after His people, protecting them and keeping them close to Himself. And giving them peace.

Action!

A) Rejoice! Get excited about what God has done for you. Reading John 3 v 16-21 should help you get excited about God.

B) Think of how you can be more gentle and considerate to people around you.

Pray!

Ask God to help you do those things. Now tell Him about any worries you have. Ask Him to give you peace about them.

Pure thoughts

Philippians 4 v 8-9

What's the last thing you read?

_____

_____

Watched?

_____

_____

Listened to?

_____

_____

Thought about?

_____

_____

WEIRD WORDS

Noble
Good and godly

Admirable
Deserving our respect

Praiseworthy
Deserving praise

Read Philippians 4 v 8-9

In the wordsearch, find some of the key words from verse 8.

P	C	B	Z	R	I	G	H	T
R	S	T	J	A	V	J	G	Q
A	D	M	I	R	A	B	L	E
I	K	H	U	J	M	F	T	K
S	P	D	X	H	Y	O	V	C
E	X	C	E	L	L	E	N	T
W	G	E	P	O	S	L	R	S
O	U	G	Y	V	L	E	U	F
R	Q	T	O	E	N	D	E	P
T	B	R	N	L	D	F	C	U
H	M	U	B	Y	A	R	X	R
Y	N	E	K	N	O	B	L	E

T_____

N_____

R_____

P_____

L_____

A_____

E_____

P_____

Read through your answers. We should think about stuff that's like that. These are the things to fill our minds with.

Time to be honest! From these five phrases, pick one for each sentence below.

all   most

some

little   none

_____ of what I read is noble

_____ of what I watch is clean

_____ of what I listen to is pure

_____ of what I think about is pure, noble and excellent

We're often bombarded with stuff that is the opposite of this — gossipy, disgusting, offensive. It's really easy to let these things fill our minds and affect the way we think and act.

Action!
What will you do to make your thoughts purer and more godly? Tick some of these...

Stop watching that TV prog ☐

Read the Bible more often ☐

Stop listening to certain music ☐

Meet up with other Christians ☐

Put a content filter on internet ☐

Spend more time praying ☐

Pray!

Ask God to help you do those things, so that what you think about pleases Him.

Content page

Philippians 4 v 10-13

Paul is still writing to the Christians in Philippi.

He has some more awesome advice for both them and us.

WEIRD WORDS

Renewed your concern
They'd written to Paul again and sent him gifts

Content
Satisfied with what he's got

Think!

Which of these things would you really like to have?

Choose as many as you want.

cooler clothes ☐

bigger house ☐

more money ☐

smartphone ☐

a horse ☐

more friends ☐

Think again!

How content are you with the stuff you've got? Be honest.

very content ☐

quite happy ☐

not very content ☐

really cheesed off ☐

Read Philippians 4 v 10-12

Paul was thankful to the Philippians for their support and money gifts. But even when he was poor, Paul had learned to be **content** with what he had.

*Fill in the missing letters to show **when** Paul was content.*

Whatever the ☐ ircumstances

With lots of f ☐ od

or hu ☐ gry

in all ☐ hings

and in ☐ very situation

in ☐ eed

with plen ☐ y of things

⬇

Paul was

☐ ☐ ☐ ☐ ☐ ☐ ☐

whatever the situation!

Read verse 13

I CAN DO ALL THIS THROUGH HIM WHO GIVES ME STRENGTH

Wow!

Paul couldn't do it on his own. It was JESUS who helped him to be content. We need Jesus in our lives; then we can be happy with what we've got.

Pray!

Ask Jesus to help you be content with what you've got and to stop wishing you had more stuff.

43

**Philippians
4 v 14-23**

*At the end
of his letter,
Paul thanks his
friends for their
generous gifts.*

WEIRD WORDS

**Acquaintance
with the gospel**
When they first
heard about Jesus

Macedonia
What is now
northern Greece

Thessalonica
City in Macedonia

Epaphroditus
The man who took
their gifts to Paul

Fragrant
Pleasing, like
something that
smells nice

Thanks and bye!

Read Philippians 4 v 14-18

The Christians in Philippi had
supported Paul's work as he told
people about Jesus. They sent him
money and encouragement. Even
when no one else did!

Think!

Do you know anyone who tells
people about Jesus?

Maybe a missionary?

Action!

How can you support their work?
Could you give them some of your
pocket money?

Send an encouraging email?

_____

_____

_____

_____

_____

_____

It pleases God when we support
Christian workers.

Read verse 19

*Cross out all the Bs, Qs, Ps to reveal
what Paul said.*

BBGQQODWPPILLMQ
BEETALQLYOBPURNEPED
SACCQQORDINPGTOTBHE
RICQPHESOQFHIPSGLBORY
IQNCHBBRISQTJEPSUSB

↓

G_____

_____

_____

_____

_____

Wow!

God looks after Christians
and gives them everything they
need. He even sent Jesus to rescue
them from sin!
How awesome is that?!!

Read verses 20-23

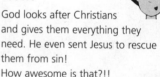

Pray!

Thank God for Paul's letter to the
Philippians. Now look back at the
Action! boxes on days 32, 41 and
43. Ask God to help you to do
the things you wrote down. Then
do them!

44

Jacob: Changed cheat

Genesis 29 v 1-8

It's been a few weeks since we saw Jacob off on his long journey from Beersheba to Harran.

Do you remember why he left home?

(Look back to day 9 if you've got the memory of a goldfish!)

Use the words in the centre to fill in what's happened so far.

At home in Beersheba

Jacob had deceived his father I___________ and c_______________ his brother E________ out of his b_______________ (see Day 9). Esau wanted to k________ Jacob. So their mother R_______________ sent Jacob to his Uncle L__________, who lived hundreds of m_________ away in H__________.

↓

In Bethel

Jacob stopped to r_______ at B____________ and had a d___________. In it God made 4 great p__________ to Jacob's family (Gen 28v15)

1. He'd give them l________
2. Jacob would have loads of d_________________
3. All nations would be b_____________ by Jacob's family.
4. God promised always to be with Jacob and p_____________ him.

Bethel blessed blessing cheated descendants dream Esau Harran

Isaac kill Laban land miles promises protect Rachel Rebekah rest

Next stop... Harran.

Read Genesis 29 v 1-3

At last, Jacob arrived. Straight away he spotted some local shepherd types who might be able to point him in the direction of his Uncle Laban.

Read verses 4-8

Who was on her way to the well?

Nice one! Jacob got to meet one of Laban's daughters. This might even be the wife God has in store for him.

Wow!

God was already keeping His promise to Jacob, that He would be with Jacob and protect him. Awesome.

Pray!

Thank God that He always keeps His promises. And that He's always with His people.

WEIRD WORDS

Pasture
Land where sheep can eat

Wife sentence

Genesis 29 v 9-20

A space shuttle takes off from Cape Canaveral in Florida, USA.

It's going to circle the earth before docking with the space station that's up there somewhere in orbit.

A long chain of events has to take place for the mission to be successful.

A safe docking depends on perfect timing. Both the shuttle and space station have to be at the same place at the same moment. The scientists and engineers need great skill to achieve this.

It's not just a coincidence.

After a very long journey, Jacob was about to dock with his Uncle Laban's family.

Read Genesis 29 v 9-14

What if... Jacob had gone to the wrong well?

What if... Uncle Laban hadn't liked Jacob?

What if... Jacob had arrived one hour later?

But he didn't! Why not?
a) Jacob had planned it brilliantly ☐
b) Just coincidence ☐
c) God was in control ☐

WEIRD WORDS

Embraced
Hugged

Flesh & blood
Family relatives

GOD WAS IN TOTAL CONTROL!

Jacob was welcomed into Laban's home and he decided to stay. Why do you think Jacob was so keen to stay?

He loved being a shepherd ☐
He fell in love with Rachel ☐
He fell into a well ☐

Read verses 14-20

Jacob's father had told him to find a wife from Laban's daughters. And God had provided just the girl he wanted to marry! Another example of God's perfect timing. But he had to work 7 years first!

Think!

When things *just* happen to work out for you, do you think *"What a great coincidence"*? Or do you thank God that He's in control of everything?

Pray!

On spare paper, write down some of the things that have gone right for you recently (maybe something at school, or a good time with friends).
Now spend time thanking God for each one of them!

Wife swap

46

*Genesis
29 v 21-30*

George was
messing around
with his ball
in the garden
and...

...you've
guessed it...

...he booted
it straight at
the house and
smashed the
kitchen window.

Uh-oh.

> **George, you're not getting any pocket money till you've paid for that window.**

Fair's fair. He only got what he deserved.

Remember how Jacob **deceived** both his dad (Isaac) and his brother (Esau), so he could receive Esau's blessing and inheritance? (It's in Genesis chapter 27.) Well, now Jacob's going to get what he deserves...

Read Genesis 29 v 21-24

Jacob had worked for 7 whole years to be able to marry Rachel, Uncle Laban's younger (and most gorgeous) daughter.

> What a massive shock when he discovered that he'd been tricked into marrying her sister Leah instead!

Maybe Jacob now realised how Isaac and Esau felt when he'd deceived them all those years ago.

Read verses 25-30

Laban was even more cunning than Jacob. He tricked Jacob into marrying both his daughters and working for twice as long!

Now Jacob had to care for ⬜ wives, ⬜ maids, and work for a total of ⬜ years. He must have really loved Rachel!

Wow!

Flick back to Day 44 and find promise number 2. God promised Jacob loads of descendants. And with two new wives, he was bound to have a big family. God was keeping His promise.

Pray!

Thank God that He's so good to His people (Christians) that even bad things turn out for their good. God is in control!

47

Genesis 29 v 31-35

Laban tricked Jacob into working for him for 14 years.

And into marrying both his daughters: Rachel & Leah.

Jacob loved Rachel, but Leah felt unloved. Awww.

WEIRD WORDS

Conceive
Get pregnant

Read Genesis 29 v 31

Why did God make it possible for Leah to have children? Go back a letter to find out (B=A, C=B, D=C).

I F   T B X

U I B U   M F B I

X B T   O P U

M P W F E

Wow!

God knows how we're feeling. He sees when we're feeling down. And He wants to help. Do you ever talk to God about how you're feeling?

Read verses 32-33

What did Leah call her sons?

S F V C F O

&

T J N F P O

Reuben means *"God has seen my misery"*. Simeon means *"God heard"*. Leah realised that God had made it possible for her to have two sons.

So she thanked Him. But she was still sad that Jacob didn't love her.

Read verses 34-35

What did she call these sons?

M F W J   &

K V E B I

Levi means *"attached"* and Judah means *"praise"*. Leah was upset that Jacob didn't love her, but she still praised God for giving her 4 sons.

Pray!

Even when we're feeling down, there's still LOADS we can thank God for. Think of some of those things, and start thanking God right now...

Trouble and strife

Genesis 30 v 1-24

We've got loads to read today, so let's get started.

WEIRD WORDS

Vindicated
Proved to be right

Plea
Cry for help

Dan
Means *proved right*

Naphtali
Means *struggle*

Gad
Means *luck*

Asher
Means *happy*

Issachar
Means *reward*

Zebulun
Means *honour*

Joseph
Means *may he add*

Read Genesis 30 v 1-8
and fill in the gaps.

Jacob married both R_____ and L_____. Jacob loved Rachel, but God gave Leah four s_____. Rachel was very j_____ and so she got her servant B_____ to sleep with Jacob. Bilhah had two sons called D_____ and N_____.

Instead of talking to God and trusting Him to sort things out, Rachel took things into her own hands. She let anger and jealousy get the better of her.

Read verses 9-13

Now Leah got jealous. She gave her servant Z_____ to Jacob. Zilpah also had two sons, called G_____ and A_____.

Read verses 14-16

Rachel bought some m_____ plants from Leah. She thought they were magic and that if she ate them, she would become pregnant! Rachel trusted in magic instead of asking God to help her.

Think!

When you have problems, where do you turn first? Friends? Family? Do you try to sort it out yourself? Or do you ask God to help you?

Read verses 17-24

God gave Leah two more sons. She called them I_____ and Z_____. She also had a daughter called D_____. Then God remembered R_____ (v22). And he gave her a son, called J_____.

Pray!

God was so good to these people even though they didn't deserve it. Thank God for loving you even when you don't deserve it.

Sheep and cheerful

Genesis 30 v 25-43

Jacob now has 2 wives and 12 children to support.

He's worked for Laban for 14 years and now he wants to go back home.

WEIRD WORDS

Divination
Using magic to make decisions

Livestock
Sheep and goats

Household
Family

Testify
Give evidence

Prosperous
Rich

All of today's missing words can be found in the wordsearch.

```
C S P O T T E D A N F
H H Y L A H R R I C H
E C I O B R E X E S O
A Z P L J E M D J D M
T M H O D E O K L T E
L E S M N R V B A R K
S P E C K L E D M O G
O Q I G T A D N B U O
N V B C U B P G S G A
S H A S T A Y K F H T
R S B R A N C H E S S
```

Read Genesis 30 v 25-33

Jacob asked L_____ to let him go h_____ with his wives and c_____.

Laban wanted Jacob to s_____ and asked what he wanted paying. Jacob agreed to stay if Laban gave him all the g_____ and sheep that were s_____ or s_____.

Read verses 34-36

Laban tried to ch_____ Jacob. He r_____ all the speckled and spotted goats and l_____, and gave them to his s_____. Laban then travelled for t_____ days to get away from Jacob!

Think!

Are you ever tempted to lie or cheat? Lying to your parents to make life easier for yourself? Cheating with tests or homework? Tell God about it and say SORRY to Him.

Skim read verses 37-43

Jacob grabbed some tree b_____, peeled off the b_____ and put them in the animals' drinking t_____. The sheep and goats drank the water and all their b_____ were speckled or spotted! Jacob was now very r_____

Sounds like magic. But tomorrow we'll see that **God** was behind it all. He was keeping His promise to look after Jacob.

Pray!

Thank God for looking after you. Ask Him to help you be more honest with people.

Grab it and run!

**Genesis
31 v 1-21**

*Jacob is fed
up with Laban
cheating him.*

*He wants to
go home to be
near his parents.*

WEIRD WORDS

**Anointed a
pillar (at Bethel)**
That's where God
spoke to Jacob in a
dream. Jacob left a
stone pillar there to
show it was God's
place (see Days 11
& 12)

Father's estate
Everything Laban
owned

Household gods
Small statues of
fake gods

Read Genesis 31 v 1-9

Laban kept trying to cheat Jacob
out of his wages, yet Jacob just
got richer and richer! *Shade in the
sheep to fit in with verse 8.*

If Laban
gave Jacob
wages of

then all the
new lambs
were

But if Laban
changed the
wages to

then all the
lambs were

Whatever Laban did, Jacob ended
up with larger and healthier flocks
than his uncle.

*What did Jacob say was the reason
for this? Unjumble the anagrams.*

G_____ H_____ B_____
  ODG   SHA   NEBE

W_____ M____ (v5)
 HTIW   EM

Read verses 10-13

God spoke to Jacob in a dream.
He let Jacob know that He was
protecting Him from Laban.

God told Jacob to go back to his
parents' country.

Read verses 14-18

THE RIGHT THING

Rachel and Leah were happy to
go with Jacob, because their dad
had been so rotten. And they were
obeying God's orders to leave
Laban.

Read verses 19-21

THE WRONG THING

They didn't trust God to look after
them. Rachel stole and relied on
fake gods to help her. And Jacob
went back to his old deceiving ways.

Think!

Do you ever do things your own
way instead of trusting God to help
you? Or maybe you can't help going
back to your old sinful ways?

Pray!

Talk to God about it right now.
Ask Him to help you to trust Him
more and to turn your back on
your old ways.

51

**Genesis
31 v 22-55**

Rachel's cover-up

Read Genesis 31 v 22-30

Jacob had run away from Laban, taking Laban's daughters (Rachel and Leah) with him. This made Laban furious. He wanted to hurt Jacob (v29). But God stopped Laban from harming Jacob (v24). God was still protecting Jacob!

Laban accused Jacob of stealing his idols. Jacob didn't realise that Rachel had taken them. She lied to cover it up (v31-35). Instead of trusting God to look after her, Rachel wanted these idols too.

Laban didn't find any of the stolen items. So Jacob laid into him (verses 36-42).

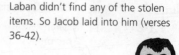

You have no evidence against me. I served you for 20 years, through hard times, and never cheated you. Yet you messed me around loads. It's only God who stopped you from cheating me.

Read verses 43-55

Jacob and Laban both had big egos. They both thought they were in the right and were most important.

Finally, they recognised that it was God who was really in charge. So they worshipped God and promised not to cheat or harm each other again.

Think!

Idols are anything we can't do without. Things that are as important to us as God (sport, friends, possessions etc). What idols do you have?

_____

_____

_____

_____

Ask God to help you make Him number one in your life, not these things.

Action!

Fallen out with anyone?

_____

_____

Well, it's time to sort it out, maybe even say sorry. Perhaps you can promise to treat each other better.
Ask God to help you. Give Him control of the situation.

WEIRD WORDS

Captives
Prisoners

Period
Ask your mum

Miscarried
Gave birth to dead animals

Fear of Isaac
God, who Isaac respected and worshipped

Toil
Hard work

Rebuked
Told off

Covenant
Agreement

Jegar Sahadutha/ Galeed
Means *witness heap*

Mitzpah
Mean *watchtower*

**Genesis
32 v 1-21**

*Jacob has finally
managed to get
away from his
Uncle Laban.*

*But he's about
to run into an
even scarier
family member.*

WEIRD WORDS

Mahanaim
Means 2 camps

Prosper
Be successful

Jordan
Huge river

Ewes
Female sheep

Pacify
Calm him down

Oh brother!

Jacob and Esau

Twenty years earlier, Jacob cheated his bro Esau out of his inheritance. Esau said that he'd kill Jacob, so Jacob ran away to his Uncle Laban's. But now Jacob would have to pass through Esau's country...

Read Genesis 32 v 1-8

Jacob was scared stiff. So God sent His angels to show Jacob that God was still with him. But Jacob didn't stay calm for long, when he heard about the 400 men with Esau! He split his group in two to try and escape.

Then he remembered God...

Read verses 9-12

Jacob's prayer is a good example of how to talk to God.

Respect for God (v9)

"O God of my father

A_____, God of my

father I_____"

When you talk to God, do you remember how great and awesome He is?

Be humble (v10)

"I am un_____"

He knew he didn't deserve all that God had done for him. And we don't deserve all the great things God has done for us.

Ask God (v11)

"Save me from _____

_____

_____"

Jacob told God just how scared he was. We can tell God how we're feeling, and ask Him to help us.

Remember God's promises (v12)

Jacob repeated God's promise to him. God always keeps His promises. This should really encourage us when we talk to Him. He hears our prayers!

Pray!

Talk to God right now, using Jacob's prayer to help you.
1. Tell God how much He means to you.
2. Thank Him for everything He's done for you.
3. Tell God how you feel and ask Him to help you.
4. Thank God that He always hears our prayers.

Want more help with prayer? To download and print your own Discover Prayer Diary, email: discover@thegoodbook.co.uk

53

**Genesis
32 v 22-32**

*It's time for the
BIG FIGHT!*

*In the red corner,
Jacob. He's
cunning, sly and
has a few moves
up his sleeve.*

*In the blue
corner, it's er...*

WEIRD WORDS

Ford of Jabbok
Shallow part of the
river, best place to
cross

Peniel
Means
face of God

Tendon
Stuff that connects
the muscles and
bones in your body

Holding on to God

Read Genesis 32 v 22-26
and fill in the vowels (aeiou).

God wrestled with Jacob!
Jacob refused to give up, so
God touched J__c__b's h__p,
so that it was too
p__ __nf__l for Jacob to
wr__stl__. Then Jacob could
only cl__ng onto G__d until
God bl__ss__d Him.

Why did God fight Jacob?

This weird wrestling match makes
Jacob cling to God. He finally
recognises his total dependence
on God.

It's the same for us!

God breaks down our pride. Brings
us to the point where we have to
admit: *"God, you have every right to
run my life your way.
Please do that."*

Read verses 27-29

God's the boss!

Jacob's new name was

__sr__ __l
What does Israel mean? (v28)

You h__v__ str__ggl__d
w__th G__d and with
m__n, and have w__n
(Jacob won God's blessing)

Giving someone a new name
showed that they now served you.
Jacob now lived for God.

Read verses 30-32

*Why did Jacob call the
place Peniel? (v30)*

**1. He s__w G__d f__c__
to f__c__**

**2. G__d sp__r__d h__s
l__f__**

Jacob finally admitted that God
was in charge of his life. Okay, he
wasn't perfect, but his life had been
changed by God.

Can you say the same thing?

Think & pray!

Think you're ok and living a good
enough life? **WATCH OUT!** God
might do something to bring you
to your knees.

Do you know you're a rotten,
helpless sinner, who's let God
down? Then **CLING TO JESUS**.
If you turn to Him, He can and
will save you and bless you!

*"God, you've got every right
to run my life your way.
Please do that."*
Can you pray that prayer?

All change!

**Genesis
33 v 1-11**

*Jacob's got a
serious limp
after wrestling
with God.*

*And now he's
got to meet his
angry brother,
Esau, and his
army of 400
men!*

*This could get
messy...*

WEIRD WORDS

Gracious
God gave Jacob
far more than he
deserved

But Jacob and Esau had changed...

Read Genesis 33 v 1-11

Circle the words that describe Jacob.

Jacob – before

He deceived his father and
brother. He ran away from Esau.
He trusted himself rather than
trusting God to look after him.
He even hid behind his servants
(Genesis 32 v 16).

Brave   Cowardly   Generous

Selfish   Deceiving   Honest

Jacob – now

He no longer hid from Esau but
bowed down to his brother (v3).
He knew that God was looking
after him (v5). And he was sorry
for cheating Esau. The gifts he
gave were to make up for the
blessing he stole from Esau.

Brave   Cowardly   Generous

Selfish   Humble   Sorry

Esau – before

He hated Jacob for cheating him.
He'd said that when his father
died, he would kill Jacob!

Calm   Violent   Welcoming

Angry   Murderous   Loving

Esau – now

What a turnaround! He threw his
arms around Jacob and cried! (v4)
He completely forgave Jacob for
what he'd done. To Jacob, Esau
was a picture of God's love and
forgiveness (v10).

Calm   Violent   Welcoming

Angry   Murderous   Loving

Pray!

Only God can change people's
lives like that! Turning lies to
honesty and hate to love.
Will you ask God to change your
life around? And maybe there's
someone in your family you could
pray for too.

Is Jake still a fake?

**Genesis
33 v 12-20**

Esau completely forgave Jacob for cheating him out of his birthright!

And now he wants Jacob to come home with him.

WEIRD WORDS

Ewes
Female sheep

Driven
Hearded/made to move

Sukkoth
Means *shelters*

Altar
Table where gifts were given to God

El Elohe Israel
Means *Mighty God of Israel*

Read Genesis 33 v 12-15

What was Jacob's excuse? Use the word pool to fill in the gaps.

altar   children   cows
die   Esau   Seir   sheep
Shechem   slowly   Sukkoth

The c_____ are weak. And, er, I must look after the young s_____ and c_____. If we travel at your speed, all the animals will d_____. Esau, you go ahead, and we will s_____ catch up with you.

Read verses 16-20

Jacob promised to meet E_____ in S_____ (v16). Instead, Jacob travelled to S_____ (v17) and then the city of S_____ (v18). That was miles away from Esau in Seir! At least Jacob built an a_____ for God, to worship Him (v20).

Jacob can't give up all of his old ways. He still wouldn't trust God to protect him from Esau, so he deceived Esau again.

Big Trouble

Doing things his way, instead of God's way, led Jacob into trouble. **Chapter 34** describes the horrible things that happened to his family while they were in Shechem. Rape, revenge, murder. In the whole chapter, **God** is not mentioned once! Instead of turning to God for help, Jacob and his family did things their own way. Which is why they ended up in such a mess.

Wow!

Don't leave God out of your life! Instead of doing what we think best, we can turn to God for help. He looks after His people, hearing their prayers!

Pray!

Say sorry to God for the times you've ignored Him. Ask Him to help you always to turn to Him with your problems and decisions.

About 30 years earlier, Jacob had made a promise to God at Bethel.

You've probably forgotten all about it.

Don't feel bad, Jacob had too...

WEIRD WORDS

Bethel
The place where Jacob dreamed about a stairway stretching from heaven to earth

Altar
Stone table where sacrifices to God were put

Drop idol

Jacob had promised that when God brought him back safely from Laban's place, he would do three things.

Promises Promises

1. The L_ _ _ would be his God.
2. He'd make Bethel into G_ _'s h_ _ _ _ _ (by building an altar there to worship God).
3. He'd give a t_ _ _ _ of his goods back to God.

It's all in Genesis 28 v 20-22.

Years had gone by and Jacob still hadn't kept His promise.

Read Genesis 35 v 1-3

Jacob's family had been worshipping pathetic statues! And Jacob had let them, forgetting God, who'd been so brilliantly faithful to him. After God spoke to him, Jacob told them to get rid of the idols. And to go with him to Bethel to worship God.

Read verses 4-7

What happened to all the idols?

Think!

What things do you think and talk about and give more time to than God? (Like stuff you own, hobbies, clothes etc).

_____

_____

_____

Action!

How will you "bury" those idols — stop giving them so much of your time, and start putting God first again?

When Jacob and his family turned back to God, He was with them in a powerful way, scaring off all their enemies.

Pray!

Ask God to help you to "bury" the things you wrote down in the *Think!* box, so that God comes first in your life.

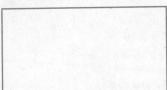

God **never** changes

57

Genesis 35 v 8-15

God had been so good to Jacob. Yet for much of his life, Jacob seemed to have forgotten God.

But God never forgot Jacob.

WEIRD WORDS

Allon Bakuth
Oak of weeping

Israel
Means *struggle with God*

Stone pillar
A monument

Drink offering
Liquid poured out as a sacrifice (gift) to God

Bethel
Means *House of God*

---

*Check out these events from Jacob's life. Stick an H next to the **High points**, and an L next to the **Low points**.*

Jacob cheated Esau out of his birthright and blessing	L
Jacob had to run away to his Uncle Laban	
In a dream, God promised to always be with Jacob	
Jacob met beautiful Rachel	
Laban cheated Jacob into marrying Leah too, and into working for 20 years	
God protected Jacob and made him very successful	
Jacob escaped from Laban but forgot about God	
Jacob met Esau and Esau forgave him	
But Jacob kept his deceiving ways	

Wow!

Like Jacob, Christians often live *up and down* lives — sometimes living God's way, sometimes forgetting Him.

Read Genesis 35 v 8-10

God reminded Jacob that He'd been given the name **Israel**. This showed that Jacob now **belonged to God**. As do all God's people.

Read verses 11-15

Jacob has changed loads. From a selfish deceiver to a man who trusts God (yet still messes up sometimes). But God never changes. He is totally reliable and trustworthy. He proved this by reminding Jacob of His great promises.

These promises were a long time coming, but God did keep them!

1. The whole nation of Israel was descended from Jacob!
2. They lived in Canaan, the land God promised Jacob.
3. Jesus was one of Jacob's descendants. Through Him the whole world was blessed.

Pray!

Thank God that He is totally reliable and trustworthy, even when we're not.

Beginnings and endings

*This is our last
visit to Genesis
for now.*

*It's all about
beginnings and
endings...*

WEIRD WORDS

Israel
The name God
gave Jacob

Concubine
Slave woman/wife
belonging to Jacob

Firstborn
Oldest son, who
would become
head of the family

**Gathered to his
people**
Joined his ancestors
in death

Read Genesis 35 v 16-20

End

Jacob's wife, **Rachel**,
died. She had wanted
another son, but died
while giving birth to
him.

Beginning

Rachel called her son
Ben-Oni *(Son of my
trouble)* because of
the pain she went
through. But Jacob
renamed him **Benjamin** *(Son of my
right hand)*. He and Joseph became
Jacob's favourite sons.

Read verses 21-26

Beginning

Jacob had twelve sons and one
daughter. *What had God promised
Jacob? (v11)*

_____

_____

God had promised
Jacob loads of
descendants. He
now had 12 sons.
They would have
huge families and would become
God's special people, the Israelites!
God always keeps His promises.

End

Reuben did a terrible
thing (v22). Jacob
remembered this
years later, and
Reuben lost the rights of being the
eldest son.

Read verses 27-29

End

Isaac died. But don't
get too sad; he lived
for 180 years! And
God had blessed him
so much. And when
he died, Isaac went to
live with God for ever!

Think!

What have you learned
from Jacob's story? (Flick
through days 1-12 and 44-58.)

_____

_____

_____

_____

Pray!

Talk to God about what you've
learned. Ask Him to help you
change so that you begin to live
more for Him.

Acts: Spread the news

**Acts
3 v 1-10**

Today we get back to Acts.

Jesus has gone back to heaven to rule as King.

His disciples (now called apostles) are telling everyone about Jesus.

Amazing things are happening...

WEIRD WORDS

Temple courts
The area around God's temple

Imagine not being able to use your legs. Try getting across the room without using your legs.

Write down some things you can't do without the use of your legs.

In Bible times, it was even worse. Disabled people had to beg to be able to survive.

Read Acts 3 v 1-7

What a gift! Something money could never buy! Last time we looked at Acts, thousands of people were changed through Peter's **preaching**.

Now he is **healing** people too. But not by his own abilities. It was by the amazing power of **Jesus** that he was able to do this.

How would you feel if you could suddenly use your legs for the first time?

Read verses 8-10

The man was so happy! What was he doing as he went with Peter and John (v8)? Go back one letter to find out.

___ ___ ___ ___ ___ ___ ___
X B M L J O H

___ ___ ___ ___ ___ ___ ___
K V N Q J O H

___ ___ ___ ___ ___ ___ ___ ___ ___ **God**
Q S B J T J O H

Think!

When something really good happens to you... do you just get happy and excited about it? Or do you remember to praise and thank God, who made it happen?

Pray!

Think of some of the things you can praise and thank God for. Now do it!

It's all about Jesus

**Acts
3 v 11-18**

Peter and John have just healed a disabled man, and he's now leaping around praising God! People were amazed.

Read Acts 3 v 11-12

Peter doesn't boast about it because it wasn't really him who healed the man. Instead of taking all the praise for himself, it's an opportunity for Peter to tell the crowd about **Jesus**.

Read verse 16

How was the man healed? Cross out the Xs to find out.

```
XXFXXXAXXXIXXXT
XXXHIXXXXNXXXJX
XEXSXXXXUXXSXXX
```

F_____

Think!

Peter told them it was JESUS who made it possible. When people praise you, do you take the credit? Or do you give God the glory He deserves.

How can you help others and, like Peter, tell people about Jesus at the same time?

_____

_____

_____

_____

WEIRD WORDS

Solomon's Colonnade
Part of the temple area

Godliness
Living God's way

Glorified
Brought honour to Jesus

Disowned
Rejected

Holy and Righteous One
Jesus was perfect and never sinned

Author of life
Jesus is God. He created and rules over everything

Ignorance
Without realising

> Thanks for sticking up for me. Why did you do it?

> I suppose it's because I'm a Christian...

Read verses 13-15

The people had rejected Jesus. They chose to release Barabbas the murderer and send innocent Jesus to His death.

Read verses 17-18

The people hadn't realised that they were killing the Christ who God had promised would rescue them. But now Peter had told them, so they **did** know. Tomorrow we'll read what Peter told them to do about it.

Pray!

Thank God that you know all about Jesus and why He had to die. Ask God to help you talk to people about Jesus more often.

61

Acts 3 v 19-26

Peter has told the people that they were responsible for sending Jesus to His death.

WEIRD WORDS

Holy prophets
Men who gave God's message to His people

Foretold
Said they would happen

Heirs
They saw the prophets' words come true

Covenant
Agreement between God and His people

Offspring
Family

Turn away from sin

All of today's missing words are in the word pool.

> **Abraham blessed cut off first Lord people Repent separated sins Times turn wicked**

Read Acts 3 v 19-21

What did Peter tell the people to do (v19)?

R_____

and t_____ to God

That means stop sinning and living for yourself, and start living God's way instead.

What happens to people who turn away from sin?

1. Their s_____ are wiped out and forgiven (v19)

2. T_____ of refreshing will come from the L_____ (v19)

God strengthens and refreshes His people. And it's a great feeling to know that all your sins have been forgiven!

Read verses 22-23

The prophets told people that Jesus would come to rescue them. They told people to listen to Jesus.

What happens to people who don't obey or listen to Jesus (v23)?

They will be _____ from God's p_____

Everyone who rejects Jesus and refuses to obey God will be cut off from Him for ever.

Read verses 24-26

God had promised A_____ that, through his family, all nations would be b_____ (v25)

Jesus came from Abraham's family. By dying on the cross, He made it possible for people from all nations to have their sins forgiven.

These people were part of Abraham's family too. Jesus had come to them f_____ so that they would turn away from their w_____ ways (v26).

Wow!

The Bible says that each of us is responsible for putting Jesus to death — we've cut Him out of our lives. But those who turn back to God can be forgiven!

True Peter

**Acts
4 v 1-12**

*Peter and John
have been
telling people
about Jesus.*

WEIRD WORDS

Sadducees
A particular group
of Jews

Resurrection
Jesus being raised
back to life

**Called to
account**
Asked to explain
their actions

Crucified
Killed by nailing to
a cross

Cornerstone
Most important
stone

Salvation
Rescue

Read Acts 4 v 1-4

The religious leaders threw Peter
and John in jail for telling people
that Jesus had died and been raised
back to life. Christians can expect to
be hassled for talking about Jesus.

Read verses 5-10

By what power were you able to heal the lame man?

It was made possible by Jesus Christ, whom you crucified and God raised from the dead!

Peter didn't chicken out.
He told them all about Jesus!

Think!

When people hassle you or question
you about Jesus, how do you
respond? Do they even know what
you believe?

Read verse 11

It's an Old Testament prophecy,
saying that the Jewish leaders would
reject Jesus, the most important
person ever!

Read verse 12

*Below, write out this amazing truth
about Jesus. (You might even want
to make a poster with these words
on it.)*

Wow!

Jesus is the **ONLY WAY** to be
rescued from sin. He died on the
cross to take the punishment for our
sin. Only Jesus can rescue us from
the punishment for sinning against
God.

Pray!

Ask God to help you understand
that amazing truth (v12). And ask
Him to give you the courage to
tell other people!

First things first

**Acts
4 v 13-22**

*Peter and
John have
been arrested
for healing a
crippled man,
and for telling
people about
Jesus.*

*Now the Jewish
leaders have to
decide what to
do with them.*

Read Acts 4 v 13-14

The religious leaders noticed two big
changes.

Change 1

They saw uneducated Peter and
John teaching amazing truths about
the Bible (v13).

Change 2

They saw that the man who had
been unable to walk for 40 years
had been healed by Jesus' power
(v14).

Nothing makes people think more
about Jesus than a Christian whose
life is totally transformed by God.

Read verses 15-22

These people refused to believe that
Jesus was God's Son and could do
these things. So they tried to stop
Peter and John from telling people
about Jesus. But P & J wouldn't stop
talking about Jesus! How brave is
that??!

*Reveal Peter's words (v20) by taking
every second letter, starting with
the top **W**.*

W__ _____ ____

____ _____

____ _____

____ ___ ____

____ _____

____ ___ _____

Pray!

Ask God to help you live for Him
more, so that people notice the
change Jesus has made to your
life.

WEIRD WORDS

Unschooled
Not taught about
religious stuff

Sanhedrin
Most important
court for Jews

Conferred
Talked things over

Notable sign
Outstanding
miracle

Pray!

Jesus was more important to
Peter and John than anything else
in their lives. Ask God to help you
put Him first in your life, so that
you just can't help telling people
about Jesus!

Shaken and stirred

**Acts
4 v 23-31**

*Peter and John
were set free
and told not to
preach about
Jesus. But
there was no
chance of them
following those
orders!*

WEIRD WORDS

Holy Spirit
God's Holy Spirit
helps His people to
serve Him

Plot in vain
Their evil plans fail
against God

Anointed One
Jesus, God's chosen
King

Gentiles
Non-Jewish people

Conspire
Plot and plan

Peter and John met up with the
other apostles and had a big prayer
meeting together.

*Find the 3 P-words that sum up this
prayer. Go forward 2 letters (A=C,
B=D, Y=A etc).*

1. Read Acts 4 v 23-24

GOD'S P_ _ _ _ _
   M U C P

They praised God for being the
Mighty Creator.

**It's good to start prayer by
thanking God that He's in control
of everything (that's what
Sovereign means).**

2. Read verses 25-28

GOD'S P_ _ _ _
   J Y L

Many people had plotted against
Jesus and murdered Him. But it was
all part of God's plan so that Jesus
could die for us.

**In our prayers, we should thank
God for sending Jesus to rescue
us.**

3. Read verses 29-30

P_ _ _ _ _ HELP!
 J C Y Q C

These guys faced hatred, beatings,
even death. It wasn't easy to preach
about Jesus! Only God could give
them courage to stand up for Jesus.

**Do you ask God for courage
to live His way and tell people
about Jesus?**

Read verse 31

P_ _ _ _ _ ANSWERED
 P Y W C P

Their prayer for courage was
answered immediately and
powerfully.

**It isn't always that dramatic! But
God DOES answer when we ask
for the courage to stand up for
Jesus.**

Prayer action!

Write down the names of people
who give you hassle for being a
Christian. Or people you find it
hard to tell about Jesus.

_____

_____

_____

Ask God to give you the courage
to stand up for Jesus!
Now make sure you do it!

Share and share alike

**Acts
4 v 32-37**

> Hey that's MINE! I didn't say you could use it!

It's easy to be selfish about things we call "mine". But these believers had a very different attitude.

How good are you at sharing stuff?

Do you keep things to yourself, with a mean look on your face?

Or are you happy to give to people who have less than you?

Read Acts 4 v 32-37

Shared everything they had (v32)

No one called anything their own (v32)

God's people

Gave to those who were poor (v35)

No one was in need (v34)

Why were they so generous?

CHOC

A phrase from those verses tells us why. Work it out by writing down every other letter starting with the top G.

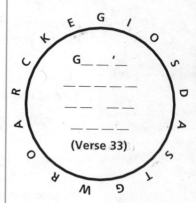

G E G I
C O
K S
R D
O A
R S
W G T

G_ _ '_
_ _ _ _ _
_ _ _ _
_ _ _ _ _
(Verse 33)

So what does **grace** mean?

God's **R**iches **A**t **C**hrist's **E**xpense

Grace is God giving His people far more than they deserve. God had sent Jesus to die so that their wrongs could be forgiven. What a gift! Sharing their money and possessions was nothing compared to that. It was just one way of saying thank you to God.

Action!

What is your attitude to money and possessions?
Are they "MINE" or are you willing to share them?
Think how you can use them to say thank you to God.

WEIRD WORDS

Apostles
People chosen by God to tell everyone about Jesus

Testify
Tell people

Levite
Temple worker

Acts
5 v 1-11

Jesus' followers were sharing everything they had, so that no one was in need.

But not everyone was being totally honest...

Lying to God

Read Acts 5 v 1-4

There was nothing wrong with giving just part of the money.

The problem was that Ananias pretended he had given the full amount. He was being dishonest.

Ananias and Sapphira probably did it because they wanted to be praised for their generosity, but they also loved money.

Think!

When you give or share things, do you do it because you want to look good, or to please and serve God?

We may be able to fool other people, but not God.

Read verses 5-11

Find an Old Testament verse by putting the words in the right places below.

looks   look

outward   heart

appearance

People _____ at

the _____

_____ but

the Lord _____ at

the _____

(1 Samuel 16v7)

God sees what we're really like. Pretending to be generous is lying. That's not really serious is it? Well, yes it is...

Read verses 4-5 again

God hates all sin. Ananias and Sapphira hadn't cared that they were trying to deceive God. But now, everyone would know how serious it was to lie to God.

Action

What do you do that you wish God didn't know about?

_____

_____

_____

It's time to sort it out!

Pray!

Ask God to help you deal with that sin problem. And ask Him to help you be honest with Him and generous to others.

WEIRD WORDS

Satan
The devil

**Acts
5 v 12-20**

What's the most amazing thing you've ever seen happen?

_____

_____

_____

_____

_____

Miracle cure

The apostles saw some incredible things happen. Today's Bible bit is full of miracles. But one of the miracles is more amazing than all the others...

Read Acts 5 v 12-16 *and write down which you think it is.*

_____

_____

Many people were healed of sickness and evil spirits. But the most incredible miracle of all is in **verse 14**. Read it again.

Wow!

The Holy Spirit is still at work today. Every time someone comes to know Jesus as their Rescuer and Lord, it's proof of His amazing power to change people's lives.

WEIRD WORDS

Colonnade
Passageway with lots of columns either side

Impure spirits
Demons that caused people to be ill

Sadducees
Rich group of Jewish people

Have you trusted Jesus to forgive all your sins?

YES	NOT SURE	NO
Praise and thank God for the amazing miracle He has done in your life	Remember that God is able and willing to forgive anyone who asks Him to	Pray that God will work in YOUR life and that you'll come to know Jesus

Do you want to know how to become a Christian? Then email discover@thegoodbook.co.uk for a free fact sheet.

Read verses 17-20

Amazing! God sent an angel to free them from jail. He told them to get straight back to telling people how to become Christians!

Pray!

God has set Christians free from sin! Thank Him for this amazing truth, and ask Him to do great things in your life.

I need Jesus in my life

68

**Acts
5 v 21-32**

The apostles were thrown in jail for telling people about Jesus. But God's angel released them!

WEIRD WORDS

Sanhedrin
Most important group of Jewish leaders

Exalted him to his right hand
Raised up by God to rule with Him in heaven

Saviour
Rescuer

Repentance
Turning away from sin

Apostles in a pickle

Read Acts 5 v 21-24

Immediately they started teaching people about Jesus again! Nothing could stop them sharing their great news!

> For a free fact sheet *Telling your friends about Jesus*, email discover@thegoodbook.co.uk

Read verses 25-28

> We ordered you not to teach people about Jesus!

But the apostles were not scared. It's true, they **had** preached despite being ordered not to. And they would carry on! They served **God**, not men!

Read verses 29-32

Peter's message hasn't changed. Fill in the gaps, finding the answers in the wordsearch.

We must obey G_____ rather than human beings (v29). You k_____ Jesus (v30). God r_____ Him from the dead to His r_____ hand as ruler in heaven (v31), to give r_____ and f_____ for people's sins (v31).

F	O	R	G	I	V	E	N	E	S	S
H	B	A	O	X	G	K	A	X	P	D
V	T	I	M	P	O	R	T	A	N	T
F	B	S	P	K	D	C	G	L	U	D
L	J	E	R	I	G	H	T	V	L	H
Q	O	D	J	L	E	E	J	E	Z	R
X	T	U	A	L	Z	B	S	D	C	R
K	R	E	P	E	N	T	A	N	C	E
A	F	D	N	D	Y	E	C	S	Q	F

Why is Peter saying all this again? Use the wordsearch.

Because it is so

IM__ __ __ __ __ __ __

Peter wanted everyone to understand why Jesus died and to realise that He was alive again!

Pray!

Read Peter's message again in verses 29-32, and thank God for these amazing truths about Him.

69

**Acts
5 v 33-42**

Carry on preaching

The apostles kept telling people about Jesus, despite religious leaders ordering them not to! The Jewish leaders wanted to kill them...

Read Acts 5 v 33-40

That was surprising. Gamaliel, one of the top Pharisees, persuaded them not to kill the apostles. **God was in control**, looking after the apostles, so that they could tell even more people about Jesus!

The apostles were cruelly whipped (v40), tearing their backs to shreds. That must have been horrible. So what do you think they did next?

felt sorry for themselves ☐

went home and kept quiet ☐

happily kept on preaching ☐

Read verse 41

They **rejoiced** and were **happy** that they were given the privilege of standing up for Jesus and being punished for following Him!

Think & pray!

How do you react when you are hassled for being a Christian? Ask God to help you to be happy to stand up for Him, even when it's hard.

Read verse 42

The apostles carried on serving God, and telling people about Jesus and how He could rescue them from sin.

Pray!

Don't back out when things are tough. Ask God to help you carry on serving Him, even if it means hard times.

And the good news?

Wow!

Jesus suffered so much more than we ever will. He suffered and died on the cross to take the punishment for the wrong stuff we've done. And then He rose again, beating death so that if we trust in Him to forgive us, we can live with Him for ever!

More from the amazing Acts of the Apostles later in this issue!

WEIRD WORDS

Pharisee
Strict Jew

Rallied
Gathered to support him

Census
A count of the population

Revolt
Fighting against the leaders

Human origin
From people, not from God

Flogged
Whipped cruelly

Rejoicing
Being happy!

The Name
Jesus

The Messiah
The Rescuer

10

Mark: Jesus the King

**Mark
12 v 18-27**

Let's get back to Mark. He's telling us about the last week of Jesus' life.

Today, a group of Jewish leaders are trying to catch Jesus out.

WEIRD WORDS

Resurrection
God's people, after they have died, will live with Him for ever

The Scriptures
The Old Testament

Account of the burning bush
It's in Exodus chapter 3

The Sadducees were a group of rich Jews. They didn't believe in eternal life after death (resurrection). And they hated Jesus Christ.

Read Mark 12 v 18-23

It doesn't seem very likely, does it? One woman marrying SEVEN brothers, one after the other???

The Sadducees thought this bizarre question would beat Jesus. They even quoted what Moses had said (v19). Surely Jesus couldn't get out of this one.

Read verses 24-25

Jesus doesn't waste much time with the Sadducees' question. *Fill in the gaps of what Jesus said.*

> In heaven, people will not m_____ or be given in m_____. They will be like the a_____ in heaven.

Of course eternal life with God won't be the same as this life. We'll have brand new bodies. And we won't be married — we'll be living with Jesus. The Bible tells us that marriage is a picture of the close relationship between Jesus and His people.

Read verses 26-27

Now Jesus has a puzzle for the Sadducees. If they reckon there's no life after death...

Why did God say that He *is* the God of A_____, I_____ and J_____? They'd been dead for ages!

He is not the God of the d_____, but the God of the l_____! (v27) Abraham, Isaac and Jacob are alive and living with God in heaven!

Pray!

Praise God if you're a Christian. Because you're going to live with Him for ever!

All you need is love

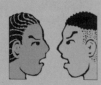

> It's YOUR turn to tidy up!

> United are loads better than Chelsea!

What do you argue about?

Loads of Jewish leaders used to argue about this:

What's the most important commandment?

They'd debate it for hours. One of the teachers asked what Jesus thought.

Read Mark 12 v 28-30

How does Jesus answer him?

Go back one letter to find out.

Love the Lord with all your

_ _ _ _ _, with all your
I F B S U

_ _ _ _, with all your
T P V M

_ _ _ _ & with all your
N J O E

— — — — — — — —

T U S F O H U I

That means loving God with every bit of you! All your thoughts, words and actions should be for God!

WEIRD WORDS

Teachers of the law
Experts on the Old Testament

Can you do that?? Can anyone?? You can't keep this command all the time. That's why you need Jesus to forgive you. But a Christian *wants* to love God.

Think!

Write down three ways you can show your love for God (praying for 10 minutes daily, trying to give up a certain sin).

1. _____

2. _____

3. _____

Jesus was summing up four of the Ten Commandments. *Tick the four which are about God.*

10 Commandments

1. **Have no other God**
2. **Don't make & worship idols**
3. **Don't use God's name as a swear word**
4. **Keep God's day holy**
5. **Respect your mum & dad**
6. **Don't murder**
7. **Don't commit adultery**
8. **Don't steal**
9. **Don't lie**
10. **Don't long for other people's stuff**

Pray!

Ask God to help you to love Him more and to do the things you wrote in the Think! box.

72

**Mark
12 v 31-34**

*Jesus was asked
what the most
important
commandment
is.*

WEIRD WORDS

Neighbour
Anyone you meet

**Sacrifices /
burnt offerings**
Cooked meat
offered as a gift to
God

**Kingdom of
God**
Living in God's
kingdom means
living with God
ruling your life

Spread the love

He said: **"Love God with all your
heart, soul, mind and strength"**.

That sentence sums up the first four
of the Ten Commandments (check
them out on yesterday's page).
Now Jesus sums up the other six
commandments...

Read Mark 12 v 31

> **Love your neighbour
> as much as
> _____**

Tick the things you enjoy...

being complimented ☐

doing well at stuff ☐

getting presents ☐

being treated with respect ☐

feeling popular ☐

If you ticked any of those, you
probably want the best for yourself
sometimes. Jesus says: **Love the
people around you just as much.**
You may not *like* all of them, but
you can still show them *love*.

What does loving your neighbour actually mean?

showing them respect ☐

helping them out ☐

giving them your time ☐

putting them first ☐

being there for them ☐

showing friendship ☐

Think!
Write down the names of people
you need to love more.

_____

_____

_____

_____

_____

Read verses 32-34

The teacher was right!
Nothing else is as important as...

Loving the Lord

Loving your neighbours

Action!

On spare paper, write down ways
you'll show love to the people
you wrote down. Ask God to help
you actually do it.

Jesus = Messiah = God

**Mark
12 v 35-40**

Today's reading is about a bit of the Bible that had the teachers in Jesus' day stumped!

Any time we read the Bible, we should start by asking God to help us understand it. So go on... do that now!

WEIRD WORDS

The Messiah
The King who would rescue God's people

David
The guy who killed Goliath

Holy Spirit
The Helper who God gives to all Christians

Synagogues
Where people worshipped God together

In Jesus' time, Jewish people were waiting for the Messiah to rescue them.

Jesus claimed to be this promised Messiah.

The Bible experts (teachers of the law) knew that the Messiah would be related to King David (v35). So they thought he was a man, and couldn't be God as well!

Was Jesus from David's family (check out Matthew 1 v 1)?

YES/NO _____

Read Mark 12 v 35-37

> **What does all that mean???**

It's something **King David** wrote in **Psalm 110**.

By calling the Messiah my Lord, David is saying that **the Messiah is also God**.

The Jewish leaders hadn't worked this out.

But we know that **Jesus is the MESSIAH**, who rescues His people. And that He is God too!

Maybe the teachers of the law didn't know as much as they thought they did! Jesus wanted to warn ordinary people about these teachers.

Read verses 38-40

Shade in the boxes that describe them best.

Greedy	Humble	Honest
Show offs	Kind	Put others first
Selfish	Hypocrites	Proud

People who are truly serving God should be like the boxes you **didn't** shade in.

Pray!

Praise Jesus that He is God! And thank Him for being the Christ, our Rescuer. Ask Him to help you not to listen to leaders who are like the ones He described.

Lack widow

**Mark
12 v 41-44**

*Okay, it's time
to put your
money where
your mouth is!*

*How much
money do you
get per week?*

_____

WEIRD WORDS

Offerings
Gifts of money
given in the temple
to be used for
serving God

Temple treasury
Room where these
offerings were
made

**How much of it do you
spend on yourself?** _____
**And how much of it do you
give to God's work?** _____

Keep that in your mind as we meet
two different kinds of people in
today's Bible bit.

Read Mark 12 v 41-42

and fill in the missing vowels.

R__CH

P__ __PL__

They gave loads of
cash to the temple. So generous!

P__ __R

W__D__W

She was scruffy and only gave
two tiny coins. Pathetic.

Read verses 43-44

The rich guys had plenty of
everything. It didn't hurt them at all
to give away large sums of money.
They still had heaps left to spend on
themselves.

*How much did the widow have left
in her purse?*

You might be thinking...

> **What a dumb thing
> to do! She could have
> bought herself some bread
> with that money. It's crazy
> to give it all away!**

So why did she do it?

**Because she loved God
and wanted Him to have
first place in her life.**

Action!

Do you give some of your money
to God's work at church or to a
Christian charity?
Is it only when you have plenty
to spare? Or does it mean cutting
down on what you buy?
Talk to an older Christian about
how you can give regularly to
God's work.

Tumbling temple

**Mark
13 v 1-8**

There are horrific wars and terrorist attacks all over the world.

They shock and surprise us when we hear about them.

But nothing shocks Jesus. He knew that all of these things would happen...

This is the temple in Jerusalem. Pretty impressive, eh? It looks so big, strong and indestructible.

Read Mark 13 v 1-2

Not one stone will be left on another!

Just 40 years later (AD70), it happened. The huge temple (and the rest of Jerusalem) was completely flattened by an invading army! Just as Jesus said it would be.

Wow!

The people of Jerusalem were punished for rejecting Jesus. The temple had been a sign that God was with them. But they'd rejected God, so He destroyed the temple.

Next, Jesus talks about the **signs** that would happen before the temple was destroyed. These are also signs of an event much further in the future: the end of the world, when Jesus will come back.

Read verses 3-8

What things did Jesus say will happen before He returns at the end of the world? Unjumble the anagrams to find out.

W_____ and rumours
s r a W

of wars. N_____
o n s a i N t

and k_____
m i n k d o g s

fighting against each other.

E_____
s h a k E q u a t e r

and f_____.
s a m e f i n

And that was only the beginning (birth-pains)! Jesus said that while these things were happening, many people would claim to be Him and deceive people. Jesus warned His disciples not to be fooled by them.

WEIRD WORDS

Birth-pains
A woman has pains **before** she has a baby. Jesus said that these disasters are only the beginning of what will happen.

Pray!

Ask God to help you not to be fooled by anyone claiming wrong things about Jesus. And spend time praying about some of the wars and famines in the world right now.

**Mark
13 v 9-13**

One day, Jesus will come back, and that will be the end of life in this world.

But before that, we've got a job to do...

WEIRD WORDS

Flogged
Whipped

Synagogues
Where people met to pray and learn from God's Word

On account of me
Because of your faith in me

Governors
Local rulers

Tough stuff

Use the backwards word pool to fill in the gaps.

> lepsog   etah   sgnik
> enoyrevE   tiripS   yloH
> draug   snoitan   devas
> yrrow   yas   dehcaerp

1. Watch out!
Read Mark 13 v 9

Jesus' followers must be on their g_____. They will be arrested and beaten. And will tell rulers and k_____ all about Jesus.

Being a Christian shouldn't be easy. We must be prepared to suffer for our faith in Jesus.

In some countries (like Turkey, Sudan and Egypt), Christians are attacked or arrested for following Jesus. That may not happen to us, but we should be ready to tell anyone about Jesus, whoever they are.

2. Tell everyone!
Read verse 10

The g_____ must be p_____ to all n_____.

The **gospel** is the good news that Jesus can rescue us from sin. Everyone needs to hear that message, no matter who they are or where they're from. Who will you tell?

3. We get help!
Read verse 11

Do not w_____ about what to s_____. The H_____ S_____ will give you the right words.

God has given His Holy Spirit to all Christians, to help them live for Him. The Spirit helps us to tell people about Jesus. Whether it's in front of kings, judges or friends at school.

4. Expect hassle
Read verse 12-13

E_____ will h_____ you because of me. But whoever stands firm to the end will be s_____.

If you tell people about Jesus, expect to get lots of hassle. Even from your family and friends. But those who stand by Jesus to the end will live with Him for ever!

Pray!

1. Ask God to help Christians who are arrested or attacked for following Jesus.
2. Ask God to help you tell people about Jesus.
3. Thank God for giving you the Holy Spirit to help you do it.
4. Ask God to help you stand up to any hassle you get for loving and serving Jesus.

11

**Mark
13 v 14-23**

Jesus is telling the disciples that Jerusalem will be destroyed.

He's also talking about the end of the world.

Scary stuff!

WEIRD WORDS

Judea
The area around Jerusalem

The elect
Christians. God's chosen people.

False Messiahs
People claiming to be Jesus

False prophets
Claiming to be God's messenger

Watch out!

Read Mark 13 v 14-17

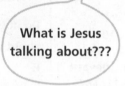

What is Jesus talking about???

The abomination that causes desolation (the horrible thing)

I'm not exactly sure what this is, but it's talking about God's temple being mistreated and disrespected. This was predicted 600 years earlier by Daniel (Daniel 9 v 25-27). It probably came true when God's temple in Jerusalem was destroyed 40 years after Jesus died.

What should people do when they see these bad things happening (v15-17)? Circle the right answers.

Take their time

Get out quick!

Leave everything and run

Slowly gather their stuff

Run to the mountains

Wow!

Some people would escape the destruction of Jerusalem. But at the end of the world, when Jesus returns, no one will escape. Everyone will have to stand before God.

Read verses 18-20

Terrible times are promised. Worse than ever before. But because of God's amazing love for the **elect** (His chosen people — Christians), these awful times won't last for long.

Read verses 21-23

*What else will happen?
Untangle the anagrams, please!*

F_____
F l e a s

M_____ will
s h e s i M a s

perform great s_____
g i n s s

and w_____
r e d s n o w

Action!

WATCH OUT! If anyone claims to be Jesus or to be God's special messenger... don't believe them! They're out to deceive you. When Jesus comes again, we'll all recognise Him!

More about that tomorrow...

Return of the King

**Mark
13 v 24-31**

The sky turns black. There is no sun or moon.

Stars start to fall out of the sky. There is total chaos.

WEIRD WORDS

Distress
Times of panic

Heavenly bodies
Stars and planets

Son of Man
Jesus

His elect
His chosen people. Christians.

The four winds
Jesus will gather His people from all over the world

Wow! What a terrifying scene. But where do you think it's from?

a) **Harry Potter** ☐
b) **Lord of the Rings** ☐
c) **The Bible** ☐

It's what will happen when Jesus returns!
Read Mark 13 v 24-27

How will Jesus come (v26)?

_____

_____

_____

That's completely different from the way Jesus came into the world the first time — born as an unknown baby, sleeping in an animal trough.

This time everyone will see that He is the **King of kings**. Everyone will know exactly who He is.

What will Jesus do (v27)?

_____

_____

_____

_____

_____

_____

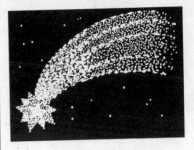

That means Jesus will gather His followers (Christians) together, to be with Him for ever!

Read verses 28-30

Over the last 3 days we've read about things that will happen before Jesus returns. We don't know when Jesus will come back, but we need to be ready for Him. Living lives that please Him.

How can we be sure that Jesus will return?

Read verse 31

Jesus' words are permanent and we can trust them completely. Everything Jesus said is true, incredibly important, and will last for ever.

Pray!

Thank Jesus that you can trust Him completely and that He will take Christians to live with Him forever. And ask Him to help you to serve Him while you're waiting for His return!

End of the line

Mark 13 v 32-37

Today is our last peek at Mark's Gospel for a while. Sob!

And our last look at the end of the world.

So buckle your seat belt and brace yourself...

WEIRD WORDS

The Son
Jesus

The Father
God the Father

Assigned task
The job each servant has been given

Every now and then there's someone in the news telling us when they think the world will end. Some even climb up mountains or tall buildings so they'll be the first to see Jesus coming! But they're always wrong...

Read Mark 13 v 32

How many people on earth know when the world will end?

So who does know when Jesus will come again?

Only God knows when it will happen. So how should we live now?

Read verses 33-37 *and cross out the wrong attitudes.*

Make sure you're ready

It won't happen in my lifetime

Be on the lookout

Do what you like

Not even worth thinking about

Think!

Which of those describes your attitude to Jesus coming back?

_____

_____

After Jesus returns, and the world ends, then comes Judgment Day.

| Believers will be gathered together and go to be with Jesus for ever! | But people who reject Jesus will be separated from God for ever in hell. |

Think!

Are you ready for Jesus' return? Are you living for Him? Are you telling your friends about Jesus, that He can rescue them from hell?

Pray!

Pray for people you know who aren't Christians. Ask Jesus to change their lives around, so they're ready for Him when He returns.

Acts: Spreading the word

**Acts
6 v 1-7**

Acts is all about how the disciples (now called apostles) began to spread the good news about Jesus.

Acts is full of ACTion!

When Jesus went back to heaven to rule as King, He gave His **Holy Spirit** to live in the lives of His followers. The Holy Spirit helps all Christians to live more and more for Jesus. What a gift!

Fill the boxes with the words from the box of the same shape and colour. This will show you what happened in the first five chapters of Acts.

Despite all the opposition, loads of people became Christians! Soon the twelve apostles couldn't cope on their own.

Read Acts 6 v 1-6

The apostles needed help with difficult jobs. These new helpers would do things like sharing out the money fairly to poor widows in the church.

These men needed to be full of the Holy Spirit and wisdom (v3).

Action!

On a spare piece of paper, write down ways you could help any busy Christians you know. Stick it on your wall and make sure you do it.

Read verse 7

The apostles got on with telling people about Jesus, so of course more people became Christians!

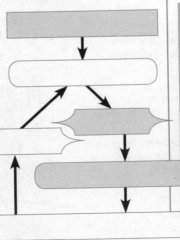

Apostles preached

Jewish rulers angry

Apostles arrested & punished

Holy Spirit came

Apostles released

People believed

WEIRD WORDS

Hellenistic Jews
Jews who spoke Greek

Hebraic Jews
More traditional Jewish people

The Twelve
The 12 men Jesus had chosen to spread the good news

Neglect
Ignore

Think & pray!

Who can YOU tell about Jesus this week?

_____

_____

_____

Ask God to help you do it. And ask Him to help you do those things you wrote down earlier.

Stephen stung

**Acts
6 v 8-15**

*It's time to
meet Stephen
– one of the
men the
apostles chose
to help them.*

WEIRD WORDS

God's grace
Showing God's great
love and forgiveness

**Synagogue of
the Freedmen**
Jews who'd been
freed from slavery

**Cyrene and
Alexandria**
Cities in Africa

Provinces
Large areas

**Blasphemous
words**
Saying stuff against
God

Sanhedrin
Jewish court

Read Acts 6 v 8-10

These unbelievers hated Stephen
doing amazing things for God. But
they couldn't win an argument
against him (v10). Why?

> **Because Stephen's**
>
> w_____ was from
>
> the Holy Sp_____
>
> **(verse 10)**

Wow!

The Holy Spirit is God. Jesus
has given the Holy Spirit to live in all
believers (Christians)! The Holy Spirit
gives us the wisdom and the words
to talk to people about Jesus.

These men resorted to dirty tactics
to get Stephen.

Read verses 11-14

- **They persuaded men
  to lie about Stephen
  (v11-14)**

- **They turned the crowd
  against him (v12)**

- **They forced him to go on
  trial even though he was
  innocent (v12)**

Imagine yourself
in that situation.
Draw how you
think your face
might look.

Read verse 15

Stephen's face wasn't worried and
miserable. It was shining with love
and peace. *Work out these words
that Jesus said in Matthew 5 v 44.*

E V O L   R U O Y

S E I M E N E

Pray!

Who hassles you?

_____

_____

Ask God to help you to love these
people and tell them about Jesus.

Stephen **speaks** out

82

**Acts
7 v 1-50**

The Jewish leaders have accused Stephen of two bad things:

1. Speaking against the temple

2. Speaking against God's law.

Stephen answered their false accusations in a long speech...

Acts chapter 7 is a quick recap on the great stuff God has done for His people.

Maybe after doing today's page you could read through the whole thing.

Accusation 1: Speaking against God's temple

Skim read Acts 7 v 1-43

It seems a bit like a dull lecture. But Stephen is actually giving a quick history of how God has dealt with His people. And he's making a BIG POINT.

Where did God send these people?

Abraham – H_____
(v 2-4)

Joseph – E_____ (v 9)

Moses – M_____ (v 29)

& E_____ (v 34) &

M_____ S_____
(v 38)

Stephen was saying that God can't be limited to meeting His people in just one building, the temple. God was with His people in **many different places**. And He still is, all around the world!

By the way, notice how Stephen talks loads about his hero **Moses**? Stephen's enemies had accused him of speaking **against** Moses. Not true!

Read verses 44-50

The tabernacle (a special tent) was another place where God met His people. But look at verse 48. God *(the Most High)* doesn't live in buildings! He is with His people (Christians) wherever they are.

Check out **Matthew 18 v 20** for one place where God meets His people.

Wow!

We don't have to be in Israel or a church building to meet God. If we are followers of Jesus, God is with us anywhere and everywhere! We can talk to Him any time!

Action!

When and where can you talk to God today/tomorrow?

_____

_____

_____

Start right now!

83

**Acts
7 v 51-53**

*The Jewish
leaders have
accused Stephen
of two things:*

*1. Speaking
against the
temple*

*2. Speaking
against God's
law.*

WEIRD WORDS

Stiffnecked
Set against God

**Uncircumcised
hearts & ears**
Not living God's way

Righteous One
Jesus Christ

Got a stiff neck?

Yesterday Stephen answered
accusation 1. Today he puts them
straight on the second one.

Accusation 2: Speaking
against God's law

Stephen told the Jewish leaders
that they were the ones who had
disobeyed God's law, not him.

Read Acts 7 v 51-53

Stephen compared these leaders to
the Israelites who disobeyed God in
Old Testament times.

Fill in the missing vowels (aeiou).

The Israelites...

• Persecuted pr__ph__ts
(v52)

• K__ll__d those who
predicted Jesus would come
(v52)

• Didn't __b__y God's law
(v39)

These Jewish leaders

• P__rs__c__t__d Christians
(Acts 8 v 1)

• B__tr__y__d and
m__rd__r__d Jesus
(Acts 7 v 52)

• Didn't __b__y God's law
(v 53)

Stephen is saying that the worst
possible way of disobeying God's
law is to reject Jesus. Because all
of God's law points to Jesus. So
rejecting Jesus would be rejecting
the great gift of forgiveness that
God offers everyone who trusts in
Jesus.

Wow!

Even though these people
wanted to kill Stephen,
he told them the truth about Jesus.
Top man!

Pray!

All over the world there are
Christians in the same scary
situation as Stephen — facing
persecution or death for following
Jesus. Ask God to help them keep
loving their persecutors and keep
speaking about Jesus.

Amazing faith

**Acts
7 v 54-60**

Stephen is on trial in front of the Jewish leaders.

He has told them they've disobeyed God and rejected and murdered Jesus.

They're not too happy about this...

Stephen was the one who stood accused of being against God. But he told the Jewish leaders that **they** were the guilty ones.

How do you think they reacted to that?

Find out in Acts 7 v 54-60

*Using the word pool, put the words that describe the **Jewish leaders** into the first grid.*

**HATING   LOVING
PEACEFUL   PRAYERFUL
VIOLENT   CALM
CRUEL   FORGIVING
MURDEROUS**

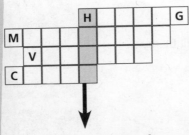

They were heading for

If we reject Jesus and refuse to live for Him, then we are also heading towards

*Now put the words describing **Stephen** into the second grid.*

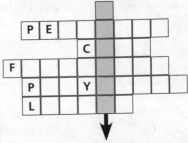

Stephen went to

If we trust Jesus to forgive us as Stephen did, God will look after us. And we'll live with Him for ever in

Wow!

Stephen was calm and forgiving because he knew God was in control. And he knew he would be safe for ever with God.

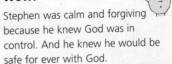

WEIRD WORDS

Son of Man
Jesus. As well as being God's Son, Jesus was a human being.

Fell asleep
Died

Pray!

If you're a Christian, thank God that you can trust Him to be with you, whatever happens.

**Acts
8 v 1-8**

After Stephen's death, the Jewish leaders ganged up on Christians, and most believers had to get out of Jerusalem quickly.

WEIRD WORDS

Persecution
Attacks on Christians

Apostles
Men sent out by God to tell everyone about Jesus

Proclaimed
Told people about Jesus Christ

Paralysed
People unable to walk

Far and wide

Read Acts 8 v 1-3

Why was God allowing this? Had He deserted His people? No chance!

Read verses 4-8

Amazing stuff! God turned the evil on its head. Persecution didn't destroy the church; it spread God's Word!

Fill in the verse numbers.

**1. Persecution
(Verse _____)**

**2. Christians preached in Judea and Samaria
(Verse _____)**

3. Many people believed in Jesus

**4. There was great joy
(Verse _____)**

This seems like an amazing surprise. But check out what Jesus said back in **Acts 1 v 8.**

You will be my...

Jesus had told His followers to go and tell **everyone** about Him. And now it was actually happening. The good news about Jesus was being spread to different countries.

Wow! 1

Today, the message of Jesus is still for everyone. Not just people we like, or people in our own town or country.

Action! 1

Who will you tell about Jesus?

_____

_____

_____

Wow! 2

Christians are still being persecuted in Nigeria, Laos, North Korea, Iran, Egypt, Nepal, Myanmar, Sudan, Pakistan, and many other countries.

Action! 2

Pick 3 or 4 of these countries. In an atlas, find where they are. Pray for Christians in those countries. Ask God for many people to turn to Him.

For more info on praying for these countries check out www.opendoorsuk.org

Rotten on the inside

**Acts
8 v 9-25**

*Let's catch up
with Philip
spreading
the gospel in
Samaria...*

WEIRD WORDS

Sorcery
Magic

Baptised
See day 88

Repent
Turn away from sin

Captive to sin
A prisoner to sin.
Sin was in control
of him.

**Testified and
proclaimed**
Told people all
about Jesus!

The gospel
The great news
about Jesus

Read Acts 8 v 9-11

Many people thought that Simon
was a G_____ P_____
(v10) sent by God. But Simon wasn't
serving God at all.

Wow!

Some people today seem to have
magical powers, but they don't
come from God. Ouija boards,
horoscopes and the occult often
have the devil behind them. AVOID
THEM!

Read verses 12-19

The good news about Jesus changed
many people's lives. Even Simon
seemed to believe. These Christians
were given the **Holy Spirit**, who
would live in their lives and help
them to serve God and tell people
about Jesus.

But Simon was only interested in
receiving the Holy Spirit so that he
could become powerful and famous
(v 18-19).

Read verses 20-21

**Simon had seemed
to believe, but he was still
rotten inside.**

Maybe you are
religious on the outside.
**But has your heart been
changed by Jesus yet?**

OR

Read verses 22-25

There was still hope for Simon and
there's still hope for you if your
heart hasn't been changed by Jesus
yet. Verse 22 says...

R_____ of your
wickedness and
p_____ to the Lord for
forgiveness

Anyone who doesn't live for God
still has a chance to be saved! They
can turn away from their wrong
ways and ask God to forgive them!

FOR FREE INFO ABOUT BECOMING A
CHRISTIAN: email
discover@thegoodbook.co.uk
or check out
www.thegoodbook.co.uk/contact-us
to find our UK mailing address.

Baffled by the Bible

Acts
8 v 26-35

Philip has been telling many people about Jesus.

Now God has a special mission for him...

Read Acts 8 v 26-31

Do you sometimes get stuck when you read the Bible?
You come to a part that just doesn't seem to make sense?

That's probably how the Ethiopian felt as he sat in his chariot reading the book of Isaiah. See what he was stuck on by **reading verses 32-35**.

Sheep to the slaughter
Lamb before the shearer

In the Bible, Jesus is often referred to as the **Lamb** (check out John 1 v 36). Jesus was sent to His death, like a lamb being slaughtered.

In the bit the Ethiopian was reading, Isaiah was predicting the death of Jesus. The Ethiopian probably didn't know much about Jesus. No wonder he was puzzled!

To find out why Jesus had to die a cruel death, find the verse in the spiral. Then write it out in the box, top right.

L___ ___ ___
___ ___ ___ ___
___ ___ ___. ___ ___
___ ___ ___ ___
___ ___ ___ ___
___ ___ ___
___ ___ ___   ___ ___ ___

(John 1 v 29)

Jesus was sent to His death to take the punishment we deserve for the wrong stuff we've done against God. The Ethiopian had never been told that Jesus died to **take away sin**. Philip explained this good news about Jesus to him.

Think!

If someone asked you to explain Jesus' death to them and what it means, would you be able to do it? What Bible bits would you use?

For a free fact sheet on *how to tell your friends about Jesus*, and Bible bits you could use... email discover@thegoodbook.co.uk or check out www.thegoodbook.co.uk/contact-us to find our UK mailing address.

WEIRD WORDS

Gaza
City 50 miles from Jerusalem

Eunuch
Important servant of the Queen of Ethiopia

Treasury
Money and valuable stuff

LOOK THE LAMB OF GOD WHO TAKES AWAY THE SIN OF THE WORLD

Making a splash

**Acts
8 v 36-40**

*The Ethiopian
guy was baffled
by the Bible.*

*So Philip
explained it to
him and told
him that Jesus
had died for
him.*

*How would the
man react?*

Read Acts 8 v 36-38

The Ethiopian responded straight
away to the good news about Jesus.
**To see what he did, go back one
letter (B=A, C=B, D=C).**

$$\overline{~}\ \overline{F}$$
I F

$$\overline{~}\ \overline{~}\ \overline{~}\ \overline{~}\ \overline{~}\ \overline{~}\ \overline{~}$$
C F M J F W F E

$$\overline{~}\ \overline{~}\ \overline{~}\quad\overline{~}\ \overline{~}\ \overline{~}$$
B O E X B T

$$\overline{~}\ \overline{~}\ \overline{~}\ \overline{~}\ \overline{~}\ \overline{~}\ \overline{~}$$
C B Q U J T F E

Hearing what Jesus had done
for him had a huge effect on the
Ethiopian. He wanted to be baptised
to show that he had turned **away**
from his sins and had turned
to Jesus.

Think!

If you've trusted in Jesus to forgive
your sins, you might be thinking
about getting baptised. If so, it
would be a good idea to talk to an
older Christian about it.

Read verses 39-40

Even though Philip left him, the
Ethiopian was still...

$$\overline{~}\ \overline{~}\ \overline{~}\ \overline{~}\ \overline{~}\ \overline{~}\ \overline{~}\ \overline{~}$$
S F K P J D J O H

He was so happy to have his sins
forgiven by Jesus!

WEIRD WORDS

Azotus
A town 19 miles
away

Caesarea
City named after
Roman Emperor
Caesar, about 80
miles away

WEIRD WORDS!

Baptism

That's getting dunked in water to
show that you follow Jesus. You
go down in the water to show
that you're leaving your sinful ways
behind you.

Coming back up again is a symbol
of having all your wrongs washed
away by Jesus, and starting a new
life serving Him.

Pray!

If you're a Christian, will you
REJOICE and THANK JESUS for
rescuing you from your sinful
ways? Will you tell Him how you
feel about Him? Go on, do it right
now!

**Acts
9 v 1-19**

The Jewish leaders were trying to destroy the church and put Christians in prison.

They didn't want people to be told about Jesus.

One of the main Christian-haters was Saul.

WEIRD WORDS

The Way
Another name for Christianity

Persecute
Hassle/oppose. Persecuting Christians = persecuting Jesus

Holy people
Christians

Gentiles
Non-Jewish people

Blinding stuff!

Crack the code to find all of today's answers.

Read Acts 9 v 1-2

Saul was obsessed with destroying the church. But he was about to get a shock...

Read verses 3-9

Who stopped Saul and made him change his wicked ways?

Think!

Has Jesus changed your life? Maybe not in such a dramatic way as Saul. But has your attitude to Jesus changed?

Or are you still disobedient to Him? What wrong things do you need to stop doing?

_____

_____

_____

Read verses 10-16

Ananias couldn't believe that evil Saul had become a follower of Jesus! Saul was now going to be God's chosen worker (that's what instrument means in verse 15).

Read verses 17-19
and fill in what happened.

Saul could

He was filled with the

God gave His Spirit to help Saul live for God.

Saul was

To show that he really had been changed by Jesus.

Pray!

Have you become a Christian yet? If not, will you ask God to change your life around, as He did to Saul?

A	B	D	E	G	H	I	J	L	N	O	P	R	S	T	U	Y

**Acts
9 v 20-31**

Saul had been throwing Jesus' followers in prison.

But God caught up with Saul and changed his life.

Now Saul is telling everyone about Jesus!

Saul searching

Read Acts 9 v 20-22

*What did Saul start doing as soon as he became a Christian? Find the right words from the **backwards** word pool.*

> hcaerp   nioj   suseJ
>
> selpicsid   sabanraB
>
> melasureJ   noS

> Saul began to p_____
> that J_____ is the
> S_____ of God (v20)

Wow!

When someone becomes a Christian, they're often so excited that Jesus has forgiven their sins that they want to tell everyone about it! Look at the names you wrote down on day 85. Have you told those people yet?

Read verses 23-25

The Jewish leaders felt threatened by Saul and tried to kill him. But Saul escaped in a basket! We can expect to get a hard time when we tell people about Jesus.

Read verses 26-31

What else did Saul do?

> He went to J_____
> and tried to j_____ the
> d_____ (v26)

Think!

Saul wanted to meet with other followers of Jesus. Do YOU meet up with other Christians for encouragement and Bible teaching? How could you do it more often?

At first, the disciples didn't trust Saul. But who did trust him (v27)?

> B_____

Pray!

Do you have friends who are really anti-Jesus? They seem far too hard to ever become Christians. Who are they?

_____

_____

Pray that God will change even them. Remember Saul!

Head over heals

Acts
9 v 32-43

Let's leave Saul for a while and find out what amazing things Peter is up to.

Read Acts 9 v 32-35

Aeneas was unable to walk and had been in bed for eight years! Yet Peter healed him. Actually it wasn't Peter who healed Aeneas. *Who was it (v34)?*

Everyone in the area saw what Jesus had done for Aeneas, so they turned to God! (v35)

Now let's meet Dorcas.

Read verses 36-39

Write down every 3rd letter (starting with A) to find three things Dorcas did to serve God.

QWAERLTYWUIA
OPYLKSJHDGFODSIAZN
XCGVBGNMOQAOZXDSWH
EDECVLFRPTGEBNDHYT
UJHMKEIOPLJOSROHYRK
FMVKAXCDAGEUUCJMLK
COMCTDPHAREFGS

1. A__ __ __ __ __

__ __ __ __ __ __ __ __ __

2.H__ __ __ __ __ __

__ __ __ __ __ __ __

3. M__ __ __

__ __ __ __ __ __ __

Action!
What will YOU do to serve God this week?

_____

_____

Sadly, Dorcas became ill and died.

Read verses 40-43

Dorcas had been dead! So whose power brought her back to life?

This amazing news spread really quickly. And so did the good news that Jesus rose from the dead and has the power to save people. Loads of people became Christians! (v42)

People now knew about Dorcas for two reasons:

1. **She served God by helping people**
2. **God saved her life**

Pray!

Seeing God working in someone's everyday life is a great way for people to find out about God. Ask God to work in your life so that people see what an amazing God He is. (And don't forget what you wrote under **Action**!)

WEIRD WORDS

The Lord's people
Christians

Paralysed/bedridden
Stuck in bed, unable to move

Tanner
Man who worked with animal skins. Many people thought He was unclean and stayed away from him.

DISCOVER
COLLECTION

DISCOVER ISSUE 4

Jump into Genesis to meet Joseph. Watch as the good news spreads further and further in the book of Acts. Let Colossians show you how to stick with the real Jesus. Discover the whole truth about Ruth. And see God's great rescue plan unfold in Mark.

COLLECT ALL 12 ISSUES TO COMPLETE THE DISCOVER COLLECTION

Don't forget to order the next issue of Discover. Or even better, grab a one-year subscription to make sure Discover lands in your hands as soon as it's out. Packed full of puzzles, prayers and pondering points.

thegoodbook.co.uk   thegoodbook.com